THIS JOURNEY BELONGS TO

_____

THIS IS ABOUT

_____

A
JOURNEY
THROUGH
GRIEF

FINDING HEALING THROUGH
REFLECTIONS OF GRIEF.

TAMMY GANN

A JOURNEY THROUGH GRIEF

FINDING HEALING
THROUGH REFLECTIONS OF GRIEF

Cover by: Tammy Gann
Artwork By: Tammy Gann

TABLE OF CONTENTS

ABOUT THE AUTHOR

Let me share with you my personal journey through grief and the reason for the creation of this journal.

When I lost my husband in a tragic car accident, I thought I lost all my hopes and dreams. It was on a hot summer's day in June. My husband, son, and I were travailing to turn off the water that we left on at his mom's. When out of nowhere a drunk driver hit us head-on. I don't remember much from the scene that night, because I was knocked unconscious.
I do remember waking up in the hospital with my dad leaning over me crying. When I asked my dad what happened, he wrapped his arms around me and cried even harder. What happened, I asked? He told me that we were in a bad car crash. How is Steffan, my son, I added? He proceeded to tell me that he was going to be alright, he only had internal bruises, but he would recover and be fine. It was when I asked about my husband David. He broke down and could hardly get the words out. We lost David..., he did not make it. At that moment I felt like my heart was ripped out of me and trampled on the floor, crushed. There goes all my hopes and dreams.

I was only 25 years old. How am I going to survive, what about my son, how am I going to care for him? Who will play ball with him or teach him how to be a man? How am I going to pay my bills, how can I work while being injured? I had more questions than I had answers. But wait, I am pregnant! My dad did not believe me at first and went to get the doctor. The doctor told us that this could not be true, because of the significant amount of injuries that I had sustained. In total, I received 42 surgeries after the crash. Even though the physician didn't believe that I was pregnant, later, I did a home test myself and discovered I was indeed pregnant! I got pregnant that morning of the crash, and 8 months later I had a baby girl, who I named Tayler.

Not knowing how to survive this loss, I searched for counselors to help me with my emotional pain, but nothing helped. My family became my strength that helped me move through grief. Having been raised in a home that loved the Lord, my mom and dad lead me and encouraged me through the word of God. My mom encouraged me to write down my feelings and let them out on paper, which I could not verbally communicate, and I began to journal my pain.

Many of my journals are full of my pain and the suffering that I went through. Some are just still too painful to read, even today. With much suffering and physical pain, I wanted God to use this for His good and to glorify Him.

Through the many tragedies in my life, I have found a purpose and vision, to help others walk through grief. Suffering and sorrow are never pleasant, but the wisdom and compassion that come from such events are priceless. This kind of wisdom and empowerment can't be toughed but must be experienced. I became a grief coach so that I can help others go through the sufferings of grief and help them through the pain. Even though there are still days that grief overwhelms me, I have learned to embrace those moments and call them "gifts".

My hope is that everyone walking in pain will be empowered, receive healing, and find joy once again

How to use this Journal

This is your journey through grief. This journal is all about you and the person you loved. Keep in mind that every journey through grief is different.

This journal is structured in three categories; Personal Reflections, Reflections of Love, and Devotional. There are specific questions that are given regarding your loss. You can choose a section that you want to write about or you can choose to do free-writing on the lined paper towards the back. It is important that you write something every day, even if you can only write one word.

By putting your thoughts and feelings into words, they come into sharper focus, and you can outwardly express what you inwardly feel. Write what comes out and don't be ashamed of it. Some of the things you feel may be unexpected or scary, and that's okay. By giving a voice to your feelings it will help you to identify them, take responsibility for them, and eventually, release them.

It's comforting to look back and see just how far you've come from day one. Sometimes, people may feel like they aren't making any progress at all, but when they have something tangible to look back on, it's easier to see the progress they've made.

May God comfort you and guide you through your pain.

Personal Reflections

There may be days that you
don't feel like writing.
That's okay — you can also draw,
or create something
else in the journal's pages.
It's entirely up to you it's your space.

BLESSED ARE THOSE WHO MOURN,
FOR THEY SHALL BE COMFORTED.

MATTHEW 5:4 ESV

TODAY MY GRIEF FEELS LIKE...

IF I COULD CHANGE ONE THING...

MY FORWARD MOTION PLAN FOR TODAY...

WHEN I AM AFRAID,
I PUT MY TRUST IN YOU.

PSALM 56:3 ESV

TODAY MY GRIEF FEELS LIKE...

WHAT ARE YOU GRATEFUL FOR...

MY FORWARD MOTION PLAN FOR TODAY...

SEEK THE LORD AND HIS STRENGTH;
SEEK HIS PRESENCE CONTINUALLY!

1 CHRONICLES 16:11 ESV

TODAY MY GRIEF FEELS LIKE...

I KNOW I'M GOING TO BE OKAY BECAUSE...

MY FORWARD MOTION PLAN FOR TODAY...

EVEN IN LAUGHTER THE HEART MAY ACHE,
AND THE END OF JOY MAY BE GRIEF.

PROVERBS 14:13 ESV

TODAY MY GRIEF FEELS LIKE...

I AM GOING TO _____ SO I CAN BEGIN HEALING...

REFLECTIONS

MY FORWARD MOTION PLAN FOR TODAY...

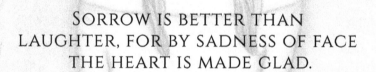

SORROW IS BETTER THAN
LAUGHTER, FOR BY SADNESS OF FACE
THE HEART IS MADE GLAD.

ECCLESIASTES 7:3 ESV

TODAY MY GRIEF FEELS LIKE...

THINGS THAT I AM WORKING ON TO HELP ME
MOVE FORWARD ...

MY FORWARD MOTION PLAN FOR TODAY...

When your heart is broken,
it might feel as if life
cannot move forward.
It can almost seem hard to breathe.
But God understands.
He wants to hear from you,
be close to you, and save you.
He loves you more
than you can possibly comprehend!
Pour out your heart to him,
and let him comfort and love you.

How good and pleasant it is
when God's people live together in unity!

Psalm 133:1 njkv

TODAY MY GRIEF FEELS LIKE...

WHEN I DO THIS I THINK OF YOU...

REFLECTIONS

MY FORWARD MOTION PLAN FOR TODAY...

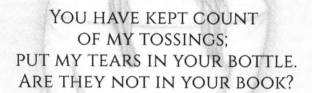

YOU HAVE KEPT COUNT
OF MY TOSSINGS;
PUT MY TEARS IN YOUR BOTTLE.
ARE THEY NOT IN YOUR BOOK?

PSALM 56:8 ESV

TODAY MY GRIEF FEELS LIKE...

HOW THINGS HAVE CHANGED...

REFLECTIONS

MY FORWARD MOTION PLAN FOR TODAY...

THE LORD IS NEAR TO THE BROKEN HEARTED
AND SAVES THE CRUSHED IN SPIRIT.

PSALM 34:18 ESV

TODAY MY GRIEF FEELS LIKE...

THIS MEMORY ALWAYS MAKES ME SMILE...

MY FORWARD MOTION PLAN FOR TODAY...

A LITTLE WHILE, AND YOU WILL SEE ME
NO LONGER; AND AGAIN A
LITTLE WHILE, AND YOU WILL SEE ME.

JOHN 16:16 ESV

TODAY MY GRIEF FEELS LIKE...

MY FAVORITE PLACE I GO TO WHEN I AM SAD ...

MY FORWARD MOTION PLAN FOR TODAY...

PEACE I LEAVE WITH YOU;
MY PEACE
I GIVE TO YOU.
NOT AS THE WORLD GIVES DO
I GIVE TO YOU.
LET NOT YOUR HEARTS
BE TROUBLED,
NEITHER LET THEM
BE AFRAID.

John 14:27 esv

TODAY MY GRIEF FEELS LIKE...

TODAY I REMEMBERED...

MY FORWARD MOTION PLAN FOR TODAY...

You don't get to go around or above your grief.
You must go through it.

DELIGHT YOURSELF IN THE LORD,
AND HE WILL GIVE YOU THE
DESIRES OF YOUR HEART.

PSALM 37:4 ESV

TODAY MY GRIEF FEELS LIKE...

HOW I CONTINUE COPING EVERY DAY...

REFLECTIONS

MY FORWARD MOTION PLAN FOR TODAY...

FOR THIS GOD IS OUR GOD
FOR EVER AND EVER;
HE WILL BE OUR GUIDE
EVEN TO THE END.

PSALM 48:14 NKJV

TODAY MY GRIEF FEELS LIKE...

IF I COULD GO BACK IN TIME...

MY FORWARD MOTION PLAN FOR TODAY...

O Lord my God, I cried to you for help, and you have healed me.

Psalm 30:2 esv

TODAY MY GRIEF FEELS LIKE...

HOW LOSING YOU HAS CHANGED ME...

I REALLY MISS ....

MY FORWARD MOTION PLAN FOR TODAY...

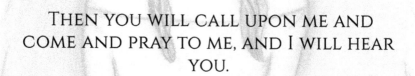

Then you will call upon me and
come and pray to me, and I will hear
you.

Jeremiah 29:12 esv

TODAY MY GRIEF FEELS LIKE...

IF I COULD TELL YOU ONE THING...

MY FORWARD MOTION PLAN FOR TODAY...

But thanks be to God, who gives us the victory through our Lord Jesus Christ.

1 Corinthians 15:57 esv

TODAY MY GRIEF FEELS LIKE...

TODAY I AM CONCERNED ABOUT...

WHAT I PLAN TO DO ABOUT IT...

MY FORWARD MOTION PLAN FOR TODAY...

I can use my pain to draw me closer to God and others.

HE HEALS THE BROKENHEARTED AND BINDS
UP THEIR WOUNDS.

PSALM 147:3 ESV

TODAY MY GRIEF FEELS LIKE...

HOW ARE THINGS GOING WITH YOUR
FRIENDS AND FAMILY...

WHAT WOULD YOU LIKE MORE OF...

MY FORWARD MOTION PLAN FOR TODAY...

BUT YOU, LORD, DO NOT BE FAR FROM ME.
YOU ARE MY STRENGTH;
COME QUICKLY TO HELP ME.

PSALM 22:19 NIV

TODAY MY GRIEF FEELS LIKE...

DO YOU FEEL THAT YOU ARE STAYING HOME
MORE OR AVOIDING FRIENDS...

WHAT ARE SOME THINGS THAT YOU CAN DO TO
MAKE YOURSELF MORE SOCIAL...

MY FORWARD MOTION PLAN FOR TODAY...

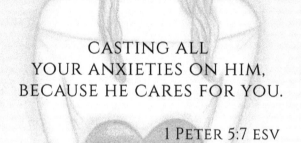

CASTING ALL
YOUR ANXIETIES ON HIM,
BECAUSE HE CARES FOR YOU.

1 Peter 5:7 esv

TODAY MY GRIEF FEELS LIKE...

WHAT KIND OF ACTIVITIES OUTSIDE OF HOUSE
ARE YOU ENGAGING IN...

WHAT KIND OF ACTIVITIES CAN YOU DO WITH OTHERS...

MY FORWARD MOTION PLAN FOR TODAY...

MAY YOU BE STRENGTHENED WITH ALL
POWER, ACCORDING TO HIS GLORIOUS
MIGHT, FOR ALL ENDURANCE AND
PATIENCE WITH JOY,

COLOSSIANS 1:11 ESV

TODAY MY GRIEF FEELS LIKE...

WHAT DO YOU WISH _____ WOULD HAVE SAID
TO YOU...

REFLECTIONS

MY FORWARD MOTION PLAN FOR TODAY...

WAIT FOR THE LORD;
BE STRONG, AND LET YOUR HEART TAKE
COURAGE: WAIT FOR THE LORD!

PSALM 27:14 ESV

TODAY MY GRIEF FEELS LIKE...

IF YOU KNEW _____COULD DROP BY AND
VISIT TOMORROW, WHAT WOULD YOUR IDEAL
DAY SPENT TOGETHER LOOK LIKE?

MY FORWARD MOTION PLAN FOR TODAY...

Pain transforms us never leaving us where we started. It won't leave you but puts you in a better place.

FOR YOU KNOW THAT THE
TESTING OF YOUR FAITH PRODUCES
STEADFASTNESS.

JAMES 1:3 ESV

TODAY MY GRIEF FEELS LIKE...

HOW DID YOU FEEL THE DAY AFTER THE SERVICE

HOW DO YOU FEEL TODAY

MY FORWARD MOTION PLAN FOR TODAY...

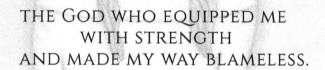

THE GOD WHO EQUIPPED ME
WITH STRENGTH
AND MADE MY WAY BLAMELESS.

PSALM 18:32 ESV

TODAY MY GRIEF FEELS LIKE...

WHAT DO YOU WISH PEOPLE KNEW ABOUT
YOUR EXPERIENCE RIGHT NOW?

MY FORWARD MOTION PLAN FOR TODAY...

THE LORD IS MY STRENGTH AND MY SONG;
HE HAS BECOME MY SALVATION.

PSALM 118:14 ESV

TODAY MY GRIEF FEELS LIKE...

THE HARDEST TIMES ARE...

REFLECTIONS

MY FORWARD MOTION PLAN FOR TODAY...

For I consider that the sufferings of this present time are not worth comparing with the glory that is to be revealed to us.

Romans 8:18 esv

TODAY MY GRIEF FEELS LIKE...

MY MOST VIVID MEMORY OF _____ IS...

MY FORWARD MOTION PLAN FOR TODAY...

COME TO ME, ALL WHO LABOR
AND ARE HEAVY LADEN,
AND I WILL GIVE YOU REST.

MATTHEW 11:28 ESV

TODAY MY GRIEF FEELS LIKE...

I HAD A DREAM ABOUT YOU...

IT MADE ME FEEL...

MY FORWARD MOTION PLAN FOR TODAY...

BE STRONG, AND LET YOUR HEART TAKE COURAGE,
ALL YOU WHO WAIT FOR THE LORD!

PSALM 31:24 ESV

TODAY MY GRIEF FEELS LIKE...

HOW I'M COPING EVERY DAY...

THE HARDEST TIMES ARE...

MY FORWARD MOTION PLAN FOR TODAY...

God uses our pain to fulfill
His purpose in our lives.

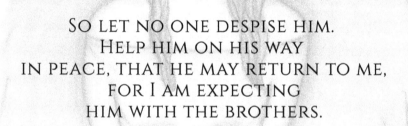

So let no one despise him.
Help him on his way
in peace, that he may return to me,
for I am expecting
him with the brothers.

1 Corinthians 16:11 esv

TODAY MY GRIEF FEELS LIKE...

SOME OF THE MOST IMPORTANT THINGS
I HAVE LEARNED ...

MY FORWARD MOTION PLAN FOR TODAY...

FINALLY, BE STRONG IN THE LORD
AND IN THE STRENGTH OF HIS MIGHT.

EPHESIANS 6:10 ESV

TODAY MY GRIEF FEELS LIKE...

I HOPE THAT...

I PRAY THAT...

MY FORWARD MOTION PLAN FOR TODAY...

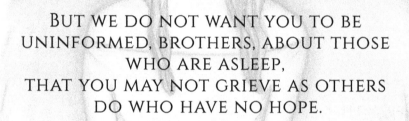

BUT WE DO NOT WANT YOU TO BE
UNINFORMED, BROTHERS, ABOUT THOSE
WHO ARE ASLEEP,
THAT YOU MAY NOT GRIEVE AS OTHERS
DO WHO HAVE NO HOPE.

1 THESSALONIANS 4:13 ESV

TODAY MY GRIEF FEELS LIKE...

THINGS I ALWAYS WISHED I WOULD HAVE ASKED...

REFLECTIONS

MY FORWARD MOTION PLAN FOR TODAY...

AND CALL UPON ME
IN THE DAY OF TROUBLE;
I WILL DELIVER YOU,
AND YOU SHALL GLORIFY ME.

PSALM 50:15 ESV

TODAY MY GRIEF FEELS LIKE...

IN WHAT WAYS HAS THIS BEEN HARDER
THAN YOU THOUGHT IT WAS GOING TO BE...

MY FORWARD MOTION PLAN FOR TODAY...

THE LAST ENEMY TO BE DESTROYED
IS DEATH.

1 CORINTHIANS 15:26 ESV

TODAY MY GRIEF FEELS LIKE...

WHAT HURTS MOST...

HOW I PLAN TO HEAL...

MY FORWARD MOTION PLAN FOR TODAY...

Let your pain be a stepping stone to
progress not a stumbling block.

AND THE DUST RETURNS TO THE EARTH
AS IT WAS, AND
THE SPIRIT RETURNS TO GOD WHO GAVE IT.

ECCLESIASTES 12:7 ESV

TODAY MY GRIEF FEELS LIKE...

WHAT ABOUT TODAY HAS BEEN BETTER
THAN YESTERDAY...

REFLECTIONS

MY FORWARD MOTION PLAN FOR TODAY...

LET LOVE BE GENUINE.

ROMANS 12:9 ESV

TODAY MY GRIEF FEELS LIKE...

WHAT'S ONE THOUGHTFUL
THING SOMEONE DID FOR YOU RECENTLY...

HOW DID IT MAKE YOU FEEL...

MY FORWARD MOTION PLAN FOR TODAY...

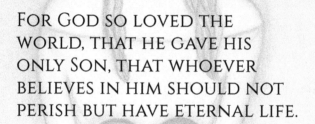

For God so loved the world, that he gave his only Son, that whoever believes in him should not perish but have eternal life.

John 3:16 esv

TODAY MY GRIEF FEELS LIKE...

WHAT MADE YOU LAUGH OR SMILE TODAY...

HOW DID IT MAKE YOU FEEL...

MY FORWARD MOTION PLAN FOR TODAY...

REJOICING IN HOPE, PATIENT IN
TRIBULATION, CONTINUING
STEADFASTLY IN PRAYER;

ROMANS 12:12 NJKV

TODAY MY GRIEF FEELS LIKE...

WHAT STAGE OF GRIEF ARE YOU IN..
DENIAL, ANGER, BARGAINING,
DEPRESSION, ACCEPTANCE

MY FORWARD MOTION PLAN FOR TODAY...

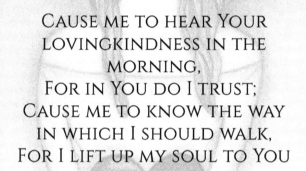

CAUSE ME TO HEAR YOUR
LOVINGKINDNESS IN THE
MORNING,
FOR IN YOU DO I TRUST;
CAUSE ME TO KNOW THE WAY
IN WHICH I SHOULD WALK,
FOR I LIFT UP MY SOUL TO YOU

PSALM 143:8 NKJV

TODAY MY GRIEF FEELS LIKE...

WHAT HURTS MOST...

HOW I PLAN TO HEAL...

MY FORWARD MOTION PLAN FOR TODAY...

One step in overcoming grief is having the right perspective on it. First, we recognize that grief is a natural response to pain and loss.
There is nothing wrong with grieving.

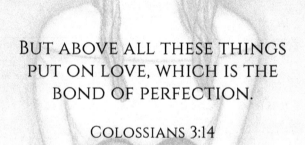

BUT ABOVE ALL THESE THINGS
PUT ON LOVE, WHICH IS THE
BOND OF PERFECTION.

COLOSSIANS 3:14

TODAY MY GRIEF FEELS LIKE...

THINGS I ALWAYS WISHED I WOULD HAVE ASKED...

THINGS I WISHED YOU WOULD HAVE ASKED...

MY FORWARD MOTION PLAN FOR TODAY...

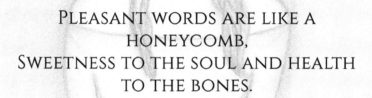

PLEASANT WORDS ARE LIKE A
HONEYCOMB,
SWEETNESS TO THE SOUL AND HEALTH
TO THE BONES.

PROVERBS 16:24 NKJV

TODAY MY GRIEF FEELS LIKE...

MY FAVORITE PLACE I GO TO WHEN I AM SAD ...

REFLECTIONS

MY FORWARD MOTION PLAN FOR TODAY...

I CAN DO ALL THINGS THROUGH CHRIST WHO STRENGTHENS ME.

PHILIPPIANS 4:13 NKJ

TODAY MY GRIEF FEELS LIKE...

WHAT ABOUT TODAY HAS BEEN BETTER
THAN YESTERDAY...

REFLECTIONS

MY FORWARD MOTION PLAN FOR TODAY...

For His anger is but for a moment,
His favor is for life;
Weeping may endure for a night,
But joy comes in the morning.

Psalm 30:5 nkj

TODAY MY GRIEF FEELS LIKE...

STAYING GRATEFUL AND FOCUSED ON YOUR GOALS
WILL HELP YOU IN MOVING FORWARD.
WRITE A FEW GOALS...

MY FORWARD MOTION PLAN FOR TODAY...

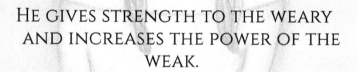

HE GIVES STRENGTH TO THE WEARY
AND INCREASES THE POWER OF THE
WEAK.

ISAIAH 40:29

TODAY MY GRIEF FEELS LIKE...

I WISH SOMEONE WOULD SAY...

MY FORWARD MOTION PLAN FOR TODAY...

Remember that feelings of grief are temporary.
"Weeping may remain for a night, but
rejoicing comes in the morning"
Psalm 30:5.

There is an end to mourning. Grief has its purpose,
but it also has its limit.

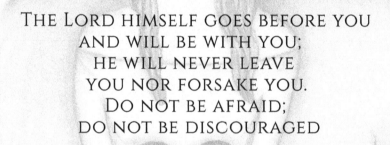

THE LORD HIMSELF GOES BEFORE YOU
AND WILL BE WITH YOU;
HE WILL NEVER LEAVE
YOU NOR FORSAKE YOU.
DO NOT BE AFRAID;
DO NOT BE DISCOURAGED

DEUTERONOMY 31:8

TODAY MY GRIEF FEELS LIKE...

HOW LOVING YOU HAS CHANGED ME...

MY FORWARD MOTION PLAN FOR TODAY...

BECAUSE, IF YOU CONFESS WITH YOUR MOUTH THAT JESUS IS LORD AND BELIEVE IN YOUR HEART THAT GOD RAISED HIM FROM THE DEAD, YOU WILL BE SAVED.

ROMANS 10:9 ESV

TODAY MY GRIEF FEELS LIKE...

HOW I WILL CONTINUE COPING EVERY DAY...

REFLECTIONS

MY FORWARD MOTION PLAN FOR TODAY...

YOU ARE MY HIDING PLACE AND MY
SHIELD; I HOPE IN YOUR WORD.

PSALM 119:114 ESV

TODAY MY GRIEF FEELS LIKE...

ONE THING YOU TAUGHT ME ABOUT MYSELF...

REFLECTIONS

MY FORWARD MOTION PLAN FOR TODAY...

Do not grieve, for the joy of the
Lord is your strength.

Nehemiah 8:10 nkjv

TODAY MY GRIEF FEELS LIKE...

THE HARDEST TIME OF DAY IS...

REFLECTIONS

MY FORWARD MOTION PLAN FOR TODAY...

So that being justified by his grace we might become heirs according to the hope of eternal life.

Titus 3:7 ESV

TODAY MY GRIEF FEELS LIKE...

THINGS I WISHED YOU WOULD HAVE ASKED...

REFLECTIONS

MY FORWARD MOTION PLAN FOR TODAY...

Reflections of Love

Like Jesus entered into the grief of the mourners in
Bethany, God enters into our grief.
At the same time, He reassures
us that all is not lost.
Psalm 46:10

He reminds us to " be still" and rest in the
knowledge that He is God. He is our refuge
Psalm 91:1-2.

He works all things together for the good of those
He has called
Romans 8:28.

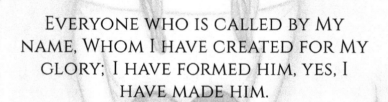

EVERYONE WHO IS CALLED BY MY
NAME, WHOM I HAVE CREATED FOR MY
GLORY; I HAVE FORMED HIM, YES, I
HAVE MADE HIM.

ISAIAH 43:7 NKJV

Today my grief feels like...

Today I remembered...

My forward motion plan for today...

BUT IF WE HOPE FOR WHAT WE DO NOT SEE, WE WAIT FOR IT WITH PATIENCE

ROMANS 8:25 ESV

TODAY MY GRIEF FEELS LIKE...

MY FAVORITE QUOTE THAT SUMS YOU UP...

REFLECTIONS

MY FORWARD MOTION PLAN FOR TODAY...

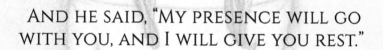

And he said, "My presence will go with you, and I will give you rest."

Exodus 33:14 esv

TODAY MY GRIEF FEELS LIKE...

TELL ME ABOUT _____.

MY FORWARD MOTION PLAN FOR TODAY...

Trust in the Lord with all your heart,
and do not lean on
your own understanding.

Proverbs 3:5 ESV

Today my grief feels like...

A random memory that made me think of you...

My forward motion plan for today...

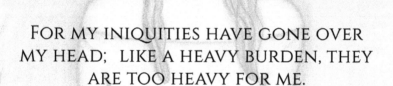

For my iniquities have gone over my head; like a heavy burden, they are too heavy for me.

Psalm 38:4 ESV

TODAY MY GRIEF FEELS LIKE...

_____ FAVORITE HOLIDAY...

TRADITIONS...

MY FORWARD MOTION PLAN FOR TODAY...

An important part of overcoming grief is expressing it to God.
The Psalms contain numerous examples of pouring out one's heart to God.

JESUS WEPT.

JOHN 11:35 ESV

TODAY MY GRIEF FEELS LIKE...

WRITE A FUNNY STORY ABOUT A TIME
YOU SPENT TOGETHER...

WHAT WAS_____LAUGH LIKE...

MY FORWARD MOTION PLAN FOR TODAY...

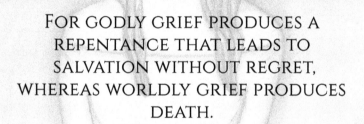

For godly grief produces a repentance that leads to salvation without regret, whereas worldly grief produces death.

2 Corinthians 7:10 ESV

TODAY MY GRIEF FEELS LIKE...

TEN WORDS THAT BEST DESCRIBE _____...

REFLECTIONS

MY FORWARD MOTION PLAN FOR TODAY...

FEAR NOT, FOR I AM WITH YOU;
BE NOT DISMAYED,
FOR I AM YOUR GOD;
I WILL STRENGTHEN YOU,
I WILL HELP YOU,
I WILL UPHOLD YOU WITH MY
RIGHTEOUS RIGHT HAND.

ISAIAH 41:10 ESV

TODAY MY GRIEF FEELS LIKE...

WHAT IS YOUR FAVORITE STORY_____
WOULD TELL...

MY FORWARD MOTION PLAN FOR TODAY...

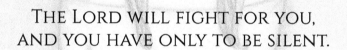

THE LORD WILL FIGHT FOR YOU,
AND YOU HAVE ONLY TO BE SILENT.

EXODUS 14:14 ESV

TODAY MY GRIEF FEELS LIKE...

WHAT DO YOU THINK _____ VALUED
MOST IN LIFE...

WHAT DO YOU THINK YOU COULD DO THAT
WOULD HONOR _____?

MY FORWARD MOTION PLAN FOR TODAY...

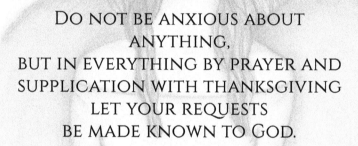

DO NOT BE ANXIOUS ABOUT
ANYTHING,
BUT IN EVERYTHING BY PRAYER AND
SUPPLICATION WITH THANKSGIVING
LET YOUR REQUESTS
BE MADE KNOWN TO GOD.

PHILIPPIANS 4:6 ESV

TODAY MY GRIEF FEELS LIKE...

ONE THING YOU DID THAT MADE ME LAUGH...

THE THINGS I MISS MOST...

MY FORWARD MOTION PLAN FOR TODAY...

Mourn with those who mourn.

Romans 12:15.

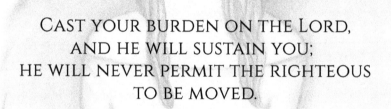

CAST YOUR BURDEN ON THE LORD,
AND HE WILL SUSTAIN YOU;
HE WILL NEVER PERMIT THE RIGHTEOUS
TO BE MOVED.

PSALM 55:22 ESV

TODAY MY GRIEF FEELS LIKE...

A FEW WORDS THAT BEST DESCRIBE WHO YOU WERE ...

REFLECTIONS

MY FORWARD MOTION PLAN FOR TODAY...

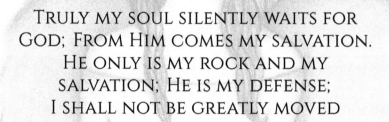

TRULY MY SOUL SILENTLY WAITS FOR
GOD; FROM HIM COMES MY SALVATION.
HE ONLY IS MY ROCK AND MY
SALVATION; HE IS MY DEFENSE;
I SHALL NOT BE GREATLY MOVED

PSALM 62:1-2 NKJV

TODAY MY GRIEF FEELS LIKE...

THE MEMORIES THAT STAY WITH ME...

REFLECTIONS

MY FORWARD MOTION PLAN FOR TODAY...

NOW MAY THE LORD OF PEACE
HIMSELF GIVE YOU PEACE AT ALL TIMES
AND IN EVERY WAY.
THE LORD BE WITH YOU ALL.

2 THESSALONIANS 3:16 NKJV

TODAY MY GRIEF FEELS LIKE...

A MEMORY THAT ALWAYS MAKES ME CRY...

I REALLY MISS ....

MY FORWARD MOTION PLAN FOR TODAY...

Yet in all these things we are
more than conquerors through
Him who loved us.

Romans 8:37 nkjv

TODAY MY GRIEF FEELS LIKE...

THINGS YOU LOVED...

I REALLY MISS ....

MY FORWARD MOTION PLAN FOR TODAY...

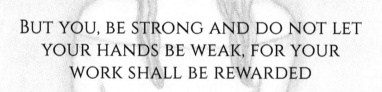

BUT YOU, BE STRONG AND DO NOT LET YOUR HANDS BE WEAK, FOR YOUR WORK SHALL BE REWARDED

2 CHRONICLES 15:7 NKJV

TODAY MY GRIEF FEELS LIKE...

A RANDOM MEMORY THAT MADE ME THINK OF YOU...

REFLECTIONS

MY FORWARD MOTION PLAN FOR TODAY...

Cling to God's promises as you
work through your grief.

"He gives power to the weak,
and to those who have no might.
He increases strength"

Isaiah 40:29 njkv.

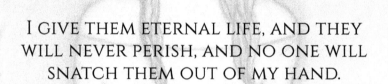

I GIVE THEM ETERNAL LIFE, AND THEY WILL NEVER PERISH, AND NO ONE WILL SNATCH THEM OUT OF MY HAND.

JOHN 10:28 ESV

TODAY MY GRIEF FEELS LIKE...

MY FAVORITE THING WE USED TO DO TOGETHER...

HOW THINGS HAVE CHANGED...

MY FORWARD MOTION PLAN FOR TODAY...

FEAR NOT, FOR
I AM WITH YOU;
BE NOT DISMAYED, FOR
I AM YOUR GOD;
I WILL STRENGTHEN YOU,
I WILL HELP YOU...

ISAIAH 41:10 ESV

TODAY MY GRIEF FEELS LIKE...

HOW YOU MADE ME FEEL WHEN I WAS AROUND YOU...

I REALLY MISS ....

MY FORWARD MOTION PLAN FOR TODAY...

I CAN DO ALL THINGS
THROUGH HIM WHO STRENGTHENS ME.

PHILIPPIANS 4:13 ESV

TODAY MY GRIEF FEELS LIKE...

ONE THING YOU DID THAT MADE ME LAUGH...

I REALLY MISS ....

MY FORWARD MOTION PLAN FOR TODAY...

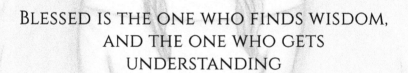

Blessed is the one who finds wisdom,
and the one who gets
understanding

Proverbs 3:13 esv

Today my grief feels like...

The little things that you did that meant a lot...

REFLECTIONS

My forward motion plan for today...

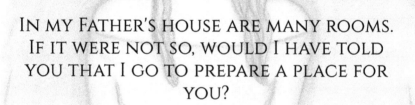

In my Father's house are many rooms. If it were not so, would I have told you that I go to prepare a place for you?

John 14:2 esv

TODAY MY GRIEF FEELS LIKE...

HOW YOU MADE ME FEEL WHEN I WAS AROUND YOU...

REFLECTIONS

MY FORWARD MOTION PLAN FOR TODAY...

Many people try to avoid pain by bottling up their emotions
or rejecting the feelings they are having.

Don't take shortcuts through the grieving process, by
not admitting to the feelings of anger or denial that usually
exist. The only way to move through grief is to move
through it. It is impossible to escape the pain associated
with mourning.

Fully experiencing the pain most often through tears
provides relief. Jesus wept over the loss of His friend
Lazarus, even though He knew
He was about to raise him from
the dead; we, too, have permission to weep.

We all experience pain in this life,
and the only thing worse than the pain of losing a loved
one is the pain of never loving or being loved in the first place.
In a way, the pain of grief
is a gift to us because it is evidence of the presence of love.

For everything there is a season, and a time for every matter under heaven:

Ecclesiastes 3:1 esv

TODAY MY GRIEF FEELS LIKE...

MY FAVORITE QUOTE THAT SUMS YOU UP...

REFLECTIONS

MY FORWARD MOTION PLAN FOR TODAY...

Devotional

Give yourself time and space to grieve.

FOR WE BROUGHT NOTHING INTO THE WORLD, AND WE CAN TAKE NOTHING OUT OF IT. BUT IF WE HAVE FOOD AND CLOTHING, WE WILL BE CONTENT WITH THAT.

1 TIMOTHY 6:7-8 ESV

TODAY MY GRIEF FEELS LIKE...

THINK BACK ON YOUR DAY, WHEN DID YOU SEE GOD...

MY FORWARD MOTION PLAN FOR TODAY...

UNTIL NOW YOU HAVE ASKED NOTHING
IN MY NAME. ASK, AND YOU WILL
RECEIVE, THAT YOUR JOY MAY BE FULL.

JOHN 16:24 ESV

Today my grief feels like...

What can you do to grow your time with God?

My forward motion plan for today...

YOU HAVE MADE KNOWN TO ME THE
PATHS OF LIFE; YOU WILL MAKE ME FULL
OF GLADNESS WITH YOUR PRESENCE.

ACTS 2:28 ESV

TODAY MY GRIEF FEELS LIKE...

WHAT SPIRITUAL DISCIPLINES CAN I WORK ON TO
DRAW ME CLOSER TO GOD ...

MY FORWARD MOTION PLAN FOR TODAY...

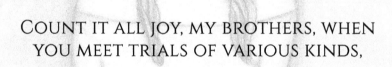

Count it all joy, my brothers, when you meet trials of various kinds,

James 1:2 ESV

TODAY MY GRIEF FEELS LIKE...

WHAT CAN I DO BETTER IN MY QUIET TIME
SO I CAN HEAR GOD'S VOICE...

MY FORWARD MOTION PLAN FOR TODAY...

FOR GOD GAVE US A SPIRIT NOT OF FEAR
BUT OF POWER AND LOVE AND
SELF-CONTROL.

2 TIMOTHY 1:7 ESV

TODAY MY GRIEF FEELS LIKE...

WHAT EXPERIENCES HAVE MOST SHAPED YOUR
SPIRITUAL LIFE?

HOW DOES IT MAKE YOU FEEL...

MY FORWARD MOTION PLAN FOR TODAY...

Jesus understood the pain of bereavement
because he experienced it personally.

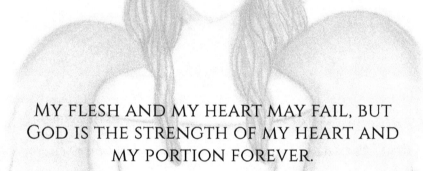

My flesh and my heart may fail, but
God is the strength of my heart and
my portion forever.

Psalm 73:26 ESV

TODAY MY GRIEF FEELS LIKE...

WHY DO I MATTER TO GOD?

MY FORWARD MOTION PLAN FOR TODAY...

BUT THEY WHO WAIT FOR THE LORD SHALL RENEW THEIR STRENGTH; THEY SHALL MOUNT UP WITH WINGS LIKE EAGLES; THEY SHALL RUN AND NOT BE WEARY; THEY SHALL WALK AND NOT FAINT.

ISAIAH 40:31 ESV

TODAY MY GRIEF FEELS LIKE...

WHAT ONE THING COULD YOU DO TO IMPROVE
YOUR PRAYER LIFE...

MY FORWARD MOTION PLAN FOR TODAY...

OUR HELP IS IN THE NAME OF THE LORD,
WHO MADE HEAVEN AND EARTH.

PSALM 124:8 ESV

TODAY MY GRIEF FEELS LIKE...

AM I HOLDING ON TO SOMETHING
I NEED TO LET GO OF...

MY FORWARD MOTION PLAN FOR TODAY...

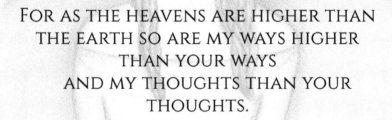

FOR AS THE HEAVENS ARE HIGHER THAN
THE EARTH SO ARE MY WAYS HIGHER
THAN YOUR WAYS
AND MY THOUGHTS THAN YOUR
THOUGHTS.

ISAIAH 55:9 ESV

TODAY MY GRIEF FEELS LIKE...

FATHER, HERE ARE SOME QUESTIONS I HAVE _____.

MY FORWARD MOTION PLAN FOR TODAY...

THOSE WHO SOW IN TEARS SHALL REAP
WITH SHOUTS OF JOY!

PSALM 126:5 ESV

TODAY MY GRIEF FEELS LIKE...

HOW HAS GOD REVEALED HIMSELF TO ME.....

MY FORWARD MOTION PLAN FOR TODAY...

To grow in the Fruits Of The Spirit, you have to
experience the exact opposite situations.
We learn to Love in unloving situations.
We learn Joy in grieving situations. Peace in Chaos.
Patience by having to wait.

As HE CAME FROM HIS MOTHER'S WOMB
HE SHALL GO AGAIN, NAKED AS HE CAME,
AND SHALL TAKE NOTHING FOR HIS TOIL
THAT HE MAY CARRY AWAY IN HIS HAND.

ECCLESIASTES 5:15 ESV

TODAY MY GRIEF FEELS LIKE...

POUR OUT YOUR HEART TO GOD...

MY FORWARD MOTION PLAN FOR TODAY...

WHEN THE CARES OF MY HEART ARE
MANY, YOUR CONSOLATIONS CHEER MY
SOUL.

PSALM 94:19 ESV

TODAY MY GRIEF FEELS LIKE...

WHAT EXAMPLES DOES JESUS PROVIDE THAT SHOWS US WE CAN TRUST GOD...

MY FORWARD MOTION PLAN FOR TODAY...

He will wipe away every tear from their eyes, and death shall be no more, neither shall there be mourning, nor crying, nor pain anymore, for the former things have passed away

Revelation 21:4 esv

TODAY MY GRIEF FEELS LIKE...

WHAT DOES CAST OUR BURDENS ON HIM MEAN...

WHAT DO YOU FEEL YOU COULD DO TO CAST YOUR
BURDENS ON HIM...

MY FORWARD MOTION PLAN FOR TODAY...

Splendor and majesty are before him; strength and joy are in his place.

1 Chronicles 16:27 ESV

TODAY MY GRIEF FEELS LIKE...

WRITE A LETTER TO GOD...

MY FORWARD MOTION PLAN FOR TODAY...

For we know that if the tent that is our earthly home is destroyed, we have a building from God, a house not made with hands, eternal in the heavens.

2 Corinthians 5:1 esv

TODAY MY GRIEF FEELS LIKE...

WRITE A VERSE TO DWELL ON TODAY...

WHY DID YOU CHOOSE THIS VERSE...

MY FORWARD MOTION PLAN FOR TODAY...

God can and does bring wonderful
things out of the darkest moments
of our lives.

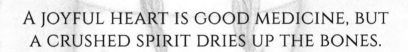

A JOYFUL HEART IS GOOD MEDICINE, BUT
A CRUSHED SPIRIT DRIES UP THE BONES.

PROVERBS 17:22 ESV

TODAY MY GRIEF FEELS LIKE...

THINK BACK ON YOUR DAY.
WHEN DID YOU SEE GOD TODAY?

MY FORWARD MOTION PLAN FOR TODAY...

FOR BEHOLD, I CREATE NEW HEAVENS
AND A NEW EARTH,
AND THE FORMER THINGS SHALL NOT BE
REMEMBERED
OR COME INTO MIND.

ISAIAH 65:17 ESV

TODAY MY GRIEF FEELS LIKE...

WHAT ATTRIBUTE OF GOD AM
I MOST GRATEFUL FOR TODAY...

MY FORWARD MOTION PLAN FOR TODAY...

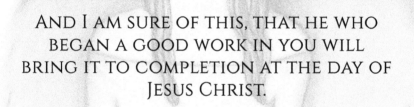

And I am sure of this, that he who began a good work in you will bring it to completion at the day of Jesus Christ.

Philippians 1:6 esv

TODAY MY GRIEF FEELS LIKE...

WRITE A PRAYER OR TWO...

MY FORWARD MOTION PLAN FOR TODAY...

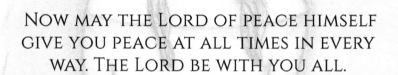

Now may the Lord of peace himself
give you peace at all times in every
way. The Lord be with you all.

2 Thessalonians 3:16 esv

TODAY MY GRIEF FEELS LIKE...

LIST ALL THE NEEDS GOD IS CURRENTLY MEETING...

MY FORWARD MOTION PLAN FOR TODAY...

The Lord is a stronghold for the oppressed, a stronghold in times of trouble. And those who know your name put their trust in you, for you, O Lord, have not forsaken those who seek you.

Psalm 9:9-10 esv

TODAY MY GRIEF FEELS LIKE...

WRITE A SCRIPTURE THAT BRINGS YOU PEACE...

MY FORWARD MOTION PLAN FOR TODAY...

Ask God to use the pain in your life for good.

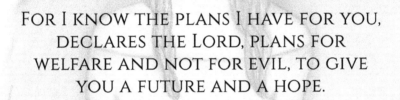

FOR I KNOW THE PLANS I HAVE FOR YOU,
DECLARES THE LORD, PLANS FOR
WELFARE AND NOT FOR EVIL, TO GIVE
YOU A FUTURE AND A HOPE.

JEREMIAH 29:11 ESV

TODAY MY GRIEF FEELS LIKE...

WHAT 5 SCRIPTURE VERSES MAKE YOU FEEL
STRONG AND COURAGEOUS.....

MY FORWARD MOTION PLAN FOR TODAY...

THE LORD lift up His countenance
upon you, and give you peace

Numbers 6:26 esv

Today my grief feels like...

Describe a time in your life where God
has rescued you...

How did it make you feel...

My forward motion plan for today...

RESTORE TO ME THE JOY OF YOUR
SALVATION, AND UPHOLD ME WITH A
WILLING SPIRIT.

PSALM 51:12 ESV

TODAY MY GRIEF FEELS LIKE...

WRITE A FUNNY STORY ABOUT A TIME YOU
SPENT TOGETHER...

MY FORWARD MOTION PLAN FOR TODAY...

YOU HAVE TURNED FOR ME MY
MOURNING INTO DANCING; YOU HAVE
LOOSED MY SACKCLOTH AND CLOTHED
ME WITH GLADNESS,

PSALM 30:11 ESV

TODAY MY GRIEF FEELS LIKE...

WHAT IS YOUR DAILY SPIRITUAL ROUTINE?

WHAT CAN YOU DO TO IMPROVE IN THIS AREA?

MY FORWARD MOTION PLAN FOR TODAY...

If your relationship with the deceased was
difficult, this will also add another dimension
to the grieving process.
It may take some time and thought before you
are able to look back on the relationship
and adjust to the loss.

REFLECTIONS

REFLECTIONS

REFLECTIONS

REFLECTIONS

REFLECTIONS

REFLECTIONS

REFLECTIONS

REFLECTIONS

REFLECTIONS

REFLECTIONS

REFLECTIONS

REFLECTIONS

REFLECTIONS

REFLECTIONS

REFLECTIONS

REFLECTIONS

REFLECTIONS

REFLECTIONS

REFLECTIONS

REFLECTIONS

REFLECTIONS

REFLECTIONS

REFLECTIONS

REFLECTIONS

REFLECTIONS

REFLECTIONS

REFLECTIONS

REFLECTIONS

REFLECTIONS

REFLECTIONS

REFLECTIONS

REFLECTIONS

REFLECTIONS

Lightning Source UK Ltd.
Milton Keynes UK
UKHW020629301222
414618UK00010B/1279

9 798512 535455

WILD WILD WESTERNERS

A Roundup of Interviews with Western Movie and TV Veterans

BY TOM WEAVER

Published in the USA by:
BearManor Media
PO Box 1129
Duncan, Oklahoma 73534-1129
www.bearmanormedia.com

ISBN 978-1-59393-689-1

Printed in the United States of America.
Book design by Brian Pearce | Red Jacket Press.

TABLE OF CONTENTS

ACKNOWLEDGMENTS

Many thanks to Michael Blake, Anthony A. Bliss Jr., Jim D'Arc, Jimmy George, Robert Kiss, Donna Lucas, Scott MacQueen, *Western Clippings* magazine's Boyd Magers, Leonard Maltin, copy editor to the stars Dave McDonnell, Lee Meriwether, Kenny Miller, Dan Scapperotti and Jeanne Wyshak.

This book is respectfully dedicated to the ones who won't get to see it: Robert Clarke, Fess Parker, Paul Picerni and Jo Ann Sayers.

FOREWORD

There is no better way to learn about individuals or their work in a movie or TV series than through a personal one-on-one interview. After reading a good interview about a film or TV series, you can re-watch it with some idea of the behind-the-scenes things that went on, and it's amazing how much more enjoyment you can derive. And no interviewer knows better, having done his research and by asking the proper questions, how to draw out of the person being interviewed exactly the proper response and the information needed than Tom Weaver.

In interviewing hundreds of moviemakers, Tom is writing and preserving film and TV history. When these actors and actresses are gone, their stories and much of the history of their films will be gone.

Nearly all these interviews were first published in my *Western Clippings* magazine where I'm pleased to have Tom interview a western-related film personality each issue, six times a year.

So sit back, relax, enjoy some marvelous Western film history — then rush to re-watch the VHS or DVD and see what you missed the first time around.

Boyd Magers
Editor-publisher, Western Clippings

Charlotte Austin
WESTERNS ARE
A FAMILY AFFAIR

Charlotte Autin's father Gene Austin and his horse Easter Bow.

Gene Austin is best known as a singer and songwriter, with the mega-hit "My Blue Heaven" the pearl in the crown of his musical achievements. But Western fans with their long memories will also remember his one fling at cowboy stardom, 1938's Songs and Saddles. *His daughter Charlotte Austin, a movie actress herself in the 1950s, here recalls her dad, his Western, some fascinating family background and her own soundstage brushes with cowboys and Indians.*

CHARLOTTE AUSTIN: I was probably five when I saw my dad's Western *Songs and Saddles.* I remember seeing it in a screening room with my father; there may have been a few other people there, but all I remember is the two of us. I was watching my father on the screen, and when I thought he flew off a cliff on a white horse straight into a waterfall, I burst into tears. And my father was sitting right *next* to me! I said, "I don't want my daddy to die!" and he said, "Honey, I'm right *here!*"

I've seen *Songs and Saddles* again since then, of course, and it's not a bad little movie for its time — and it turns out the fellow who went over the cliff was not my dad, but *his* father in the movie. My dad lost a lot of weight for that movie, he looked terrific in it, and for a guy who really hadn't done any acting, he was surprisingly good…a natural! It's the only starring role he had in films, so I was really surprised. He had a natural instinct for it. My mother tells me she was a little jealous at the time, she thought that he had his eye on the leading lady [Lynne Berkeley]!

Around that time, my dad bought a handsome Tennessee Walking Horse called Easter Bow…and from *Songs and Saddles,* he brought home an absolutely beautiful silver pistol. A long, slim, double-barreled Spanish dueling pistol, with a mother-of-pearl handle. Gorgeous. He must have just left it behind when he and my mother divorced. I inherited it, and it was stolen from my home years later.

Q: But you of all people owned it for a while?

Yes, and I *hate* guns. When Robert Kennedy was killed in 1968, I drafted a gun-control petition and in a week, with a friend, got 2300 signatures, was threatened with arrest, and was accosted by NRA members, the Teamsters and one or two rabid little old ladies. But I see no hope, *ever,* of passing *any* kind of legislation. We're the only country in the world that kills like this — not England, Japan or any of the European countries are allowed to wield this deadly weapon the way America does. This thing that happened yesterday [the April 16, 2007, Virginia Tech massacre]… unbelievable. And still the gun lobby is *so* powerful, *so* strong, that nobody will take it on. They cite the "right to bear arms," conveniently forgetting this refers to a "well-armed militia" and not the individual…

My father was born in Gainesville, Texas, and grew up in Minden, Louisiana, and he loved horses. He told me stories about how, in *Songs and Saddles,* he jumped down from a second floor saloon balcony onto the back of a horse but missed on the first couple of tries *[laughs]!* He was an

A lobby card from Gene Austin's one shot at Western movie stardom, Songs and Saddles.

excellent horseman. He had grown up with a white horse that he loved and sometimes *slept* with, in the stall. He'd be asleep and feel this huge heavy weight on him, and he'd wake up and the horse's head would be on his chest! His stepfather was a blacksmith, and *his* claim to fame was that he shoed the great Dan Patch. There was also an old story in the family that one of his uncles was a horse thief hung for thieving! There were a *lot* of interesting stories on that side of the family. Dad's mother, Belle Hearrell, claimed to have been a friend of the Dalton boys, a gang well-known in Texas. Other stories included the lore that we were descended from Sacajawea [the Shoshone guide for the 1804-06 Lewis and Clark Expedition]. It's more than confusing trying to track the history of the "Bird Woman" — she was called that because she could mount a horse bareback on a run. Her life was a mystery in itself. She married [French-Canadian] Toussaint Charbonneau and they had a child, Jean-Baptiste, who was sent to school in Paris by Capt. Clark. Jean-Baptiste Charbonneau, so the family story goes, returned to marry a woman in St. Louis and *they* had a girl, Elmancie Charbonneau, whose daughter Belle was Gene's mother and my grandmother. Belle was a character…a wily, wild and wandering woman who did a lot of emotional damage to my father when he was a boy. Maybe that's why he married five times…always looking for the ideal woman she wasn't. My father used to sleep under neighbors' front porches in Louisiana; he'd run away from home; he once hopped a freight train to Oklahoma to join a circus and ended up, sadly, selling balloons; he played piano in a "sporting house" in New Orleans; and he joined the Army at 16. A very colorful, very interesting life, but a lot of pain, a lot of loneliness connected with it. Out of it came his classic song "The Lonesome Road"…and I know that's why he could sing the way he did, with a lot of soul. There was a sweetness, a melancholy that had an especially strong appeal for women. He once told me that when I was very little, I'd sit with him at the piano and cry quietly when he sang.

My father loved Westerns, he loved reading Westerns, he loved Hopalong Cassidy. In fact, he rests now in a mausoleum in Forest Lawn, in Glendale, in the same room that holds Hopalong Cassidy [actor William Boyd]. My father would be delighted, he *lllloved* Hopalong Cassidy; he watched every old Western and especially Hopalong Cassidy. How fitting that he's in the same place as [Boyd], and surrounded by beautiful marble statues of women which would *also* delight my father! Gene Autry was his good friend. Once when I was in my 20s, I went with my father to Autry's home in the Valley, and Autry proudly led me into his huge walk-in closet and showed me every…single…pair of custom-made riding boots and hats to match. And what seemed like hundreds of colorful, beaded and fringed, specially made Western outfits. He showed me *all* of them! I had to go through every single one of them!

Q: Did this mean *anything to you?*

No! In fact, I'll tell you this frankly: I never was a fan of Gene Autry's *singing!* But he was smart with his money. My father and mother were divorced when I was six, and in later years when my dad would come to town, he'd always stay at Gene's hotel, the Continental, on Sunset. They were good friends for many, many years.

My father's dream was to retire one day and own a racing farm and breed race horses. He loved the races…oh my God, *loved* gambling and the races. And he was an avid bettor. I remember him sitting in bed all day calling his bookie, and saying to me, "Come on over here, Sharkie!" (He nicknamed me Sharkie, after a wrestler!) "Come here, Sharkie! I want you to learn my 'system.'" I was *nine!* I *hated* math and I had no interest in his betting "system." One day he took me to the races with him, and I said, "Daddy, can I have two dollars [to bet on a horse]?" "*No.* Be quiet. Don't bother me" — he was doing his "system." Well, every horse

Bowling night with Gene Austin and his wife Agnes, Charlotte's parents.

I picked *won*, including one that was an 11-to-1 long shot. He wanted to kill me: All the horses I picked, that he wouldn't give me the money to bet on, came in, winning a lot of money. Every horse *he* picked was a loser *[laughs]*, and he was so mad!

In 1943, I had a screen test that I "won" in a "Better Babies" talent contest. Somebody entered me in a *Herald Examiner* Better Babies contest without my knowledge, as usual, and I ended up having to compete. On the ride downtown to go to perform in this thing, I was violently sick, and trying to keep from throwing up, and my father was saying, "Come *on*, buck up! You gotta be a trouper!" Here I was, a nine-year-old sick to her stomach having to sing "Murder He Says," a wild Betty Hutton song, as my father, accompanying me on piano, totally drowned me out. I was singing *[she makes squeaky sounds]* in this tiny voice nobody could hear, and my father was *banging* on the piano, and I won the contest! (Or maybe it was fixed. I have a feeling it was fixed.) They sent me to Republic for a screen test and handed me a pair of knitting needles and yarn and said, "Here, pretend you're knitting." I didn't know what I was doing. Needless to say, I didn't get a contract.

Charlotte is met by her dad at a Las Vegas airport.

A few years later, I did get into movies. I was under contract to 20th Century-Fox. You know something that was very hurtful? When the movie *The Far Horizons* [1955], the story of the Lewis and Clark Expedition and Sacajawea, was about to be made, I wanted the part of Sacajawea *so* much. I told them, "But, I'm her *descendant!*," but they weren't the least bit interested. It ended up with Fred MacMurray, Charlton Heston and… Donna Reed! Donna Reed playing an Indian?? Very upsetting.

But in the only two Westerns I did, I *did* play Indian women. On the TV series *The Adventures of Jim Bowie* I did an episode called "An Eye for an Eye" where I played an Indian named Menthune. It was interesting because on that show was an American Indian guy and we were able to have some good, long talks, so at least working on *Jim Bowie* amounted to something. I had coffee with him and, from this proud Apache man, whose name I cannot recall, I learned a lot about what was happening on Oklahoma reservations. The daily injustices he and his tribe faced and their underlying feelings of despair. The only other thing that stands out was a scene with Jim Bowie [played by Scott Forbes] where my horse was eating my hair! The horse was standing next to me and I was standing next to Jim Bowie, and the horse kept grabbing my braids and chewing on them while I was trying to speak. We must have done it 100 times because he was fascinated with my hair.

Q: What's the key to playing an Indian?

Well, at that time, I didn't think about "the key," but knew instinctively not to assault the part with words. Words seemed irrelevant — and, believe me, these scripted words *were! Under*playing would have been "the key." They're very quiet people, very spiritual people. I've always held the same reverence for nature — the living, natural world — as the Indians do. We pass through this earth but Mother Earth remains constant. I work hard now toward saving the wolves in Alaska, Montana, Idaho — states that permit (or are threatening to permit) aerial gunning of wolves and are offering huge bounties for those killed. Humans could learn so much from these beautiful animals; for instance, they bond for life with one mate. And they go out and hunt [on behalf of] older wolves that can no longer hunt for themselves. We should be so lucky and have the same kind of instincts that wolves do.

Oh, and on *Jim Bowie*, my hair-munching horse ran away with me on the soundstage — I think he was trying to tell me something. When I was a child, my dream was to own a horse; that's what I wanted more than *any*thing in the world after reading *Black Beauty, My Friend Flicka and Thunderhead*. All my friends in Burbank owned horses and I was the only one who didn't, but they would loan me a horse and I'd ride with them. Every year the family would go to Litchfield Park, Arizona, to visit my stepfather's father, P.W. Litchfield, chairman of the board of Goodyear, who had a beautiful ranch there. And every year at Easter time,

spring, I would say, "Please, please, can't I just ride a horse to Arizona? You can drive and I'll ride, and I'll meet you there! We'll be fine — my horse and I can spend the night on the desert!" Ride a horse to Arizona! Well, in later years, I wished that I could have made the trip Sacajawea made. That's something I really, really would love to have done. She was an incredibly brave and resourceful woman.

The other Indian I played was in the movie *Pawnee* [1957]. George Montgomery was a rogue. A charming, incredibly handsome man, oh, yes — and he was a devil! But, you know something?, he was a lovely man, he really was, and a better furniture designer than actor.

Charlotte Austin today.

George was White Russian and proud of it. I didn't know him at all before *Pawnee*; he came to my house with the script of *Pawnee*, we went over it, he asked if I was interested and I was more than happy to play an Indian woman in a movie, *finally*. Princess Dancing Fawn, at that! Although it wasn't a very good picture, I was glad that I was able to do what I'd always wanted to do.

One scene in *Pawnee* was absolutely ridiculous: I was supposed to have been killed, and I was lying on a battlefield of some kind, without even a black-and-blue mark. Not a spot of blood, *nothing*. I'm "dead," but there was nothing there. I must have died of a heart attack! Fortunately, the scene was cut. The director George Waggner was…just a kindly, older man *[laughs]*…not the world's best director. George Montgomery seemed to oversee and direct a lot of it. I think it was George's project, and he seemed to be in change at all times.

Incidentally, I recently showed *Songs and Saddles* to my grandson Caeden. He absolutely loved it, and he wants to see it over and over and over again. Forget about *my* movies, he couldn't care less, but he wants to see *Songs and Saddles*. He loves seeing my father, *his* great-grandfather and of course he loves the action and, ugh, the guns. He's so very much like my dad, I can't believe it. He's songwriting now...sitting at the same piano my dad wrote some of his best songs at...the piano Mary Martin and Mae West sang at. He just turned seven, and he's writing great lyrics. I'm going to have to help him a little with the music, 'cause he's not so hot on the music, but his lyrics are absolutely wonderful. It's like my father has invaded his soul, he's *so* much like him. My father, right now, if he were alive, would flip over him. When Caeden and I go out, we always repeat a phrase from my dad: "Here come them showfolks, laughin' and scratchin'!" And in my "mind's ear" I can hear my dad saying to Caeden, "Come on, little buddy, let's hit the road!" I told that to Caeden, and he said, "And I'd go *with* him, Grandma!"

Kenneth Chase

MAKING UP
THE WILD WILD WEST

Kenneth Chase in 1967 with Maurice Evans, made-up by Chase to play Dr. Zaius in Planet of the Apes. *For a beginning makeup artist like Chase, getting to work on that movie was "a big deal."*

In every episode of The Wild Wild West, *Secret Service agent Artemus Gordon would don an elaborate, usually outlandish disguise in order to work undercover and/or to infiltrate the gang of the Villain of the Week. As at least one critic pointed out, all this subterfuge was pointless since no one ever recognized Gordon as a government man when he was* un*disguised. But it provided the series with its weekly dose of comic relief and kept Martin happy; he accepted the role only after being told that he would be able to enjoy the character actor's dream of a strong new role in each segment.*

In reel *life it was master-of-disguise Gordon who changed his own features but in* real *life the magic was worked, in the series' fourth season, by a young, new-to-the-business makeup man named Kenneth Chase.*

KENNETH CHASE: My wife Marylyn's father was a makeup artist; before she and I got together, I wasn't aware such a job existed. His name was Bob Mark and he had been the head makeup guy at Republic Pictures for 20 years. When I met him, Republic was no longer in business and he was working freelance. My getting into the makeup profession was his idea, because Marylyn and I were both 19 when we got married and my prospects weren't very good. At first, my wife's mother and father *weren't* interested in trying to get me into that business, for all the obvious reasons: because of all the temptations, and the lifestyle. But I guess they thought it would still be a better alternative than where I was at that time.

I was "on permit" when I first started, meaning that I wasn't a regular member of Makeup Artists and Hairstylists Local 706. But things were so busy in those days that they went outside of the regular membership to people who were related to members and had received training. The very first assignment I had was a TV series called *The Long, Hot Summer* [1965-66]; I worked for Tony Lloyd, the head guy on that, for a while. Then I bounced around doing different things, including the TV series *The Time Tunnel*, and the first big break I had was *Planet of the Apes* [1968] on which I did the makeup for Dr. Zaius [played by Maurice Evans], one of the main characters. To get to work on that movie was a big deal for *any*body who was starting out in makeup. John Chambers was the mentor of all of us [the *Apes* makeup artists] and there were training sessions at 20th Century-Fox and I guess he felt I was doing really well in the training sessions because he encouraged me and actually assigned me that plum character, which was unusual 'cause I wasn't even a journeyman makeup artist at that time. And it didn't go unnoticed by a lot of the older guys, who sort of resented that. There were little pitfalls here and there on *Planet of the Apes* but it worked out just fine. Once that movie was over, I started building some false noses and things, teaching myself how to do that, with John Chambers' help.

Prior to the start of *Wild Wild West* Season 4, I got a couple of jobs working on that series as an extra helper, when Don Schoenfeld was the head makeup guy. I kind of established myself there as being pretty handy, and when Don decided to leave the show and I heard about it, I showed

up at George Lane's office door at CBS Studio Center where *Wild West* was shot. George was the head of the makeup depart-ment, and I showed up with a jar full of false noses and things that I had made at home in North Hollywood. I guess that worked, because he gave me the show. For a young guy, which I was at the time, it was a great opportunity to get to do all those *Wild West* makeups, it was just fantastic. I wanted that job in a big way.

Ross Martin was a little reluc-tant about me at first because I was so young, only 26, which was really young in those days. In fact, he didn't know that I knew this, but he actually went to George Lane and tried to get George to hire somebody else. But that was before I actually did any of those nice make-ups on Ross. He was great after that.

Robert Conrad was kind of an odd character. He was pretty close to Don Schoenfeld so I don't think he particularly liked me, and he didn't have much to do with me. Conrad didn't wear makeup, incidentally. He was a pretty good-looking guy and had a nice skin tone, and didn't really require any. He was a little bit full of himself, but the nice thing about him was that whatever you saw was *real*. If he didn't like you, at least he wasn't somebody who went behind your back. Conversely, at least in that one instance, Ross Martin was just wonderful to *me* and then went behind my back to try to get me fired, so…you can take that for what it's worth! I'm speaking ill of the dead so let me quickly add that I really liked Ross and we became very cordial and had a very nice relationship once I proved myself to him. Ross' makeups usually involved false noses — there was always a false nose — and a beard. Ross' makeup as a Russian priest [in "The Night of the Cossacks"] was a favorite of mine because I hand-laid a long beard, which was a skill I worked very long and hard to develop. I used to really love doing beards. John Chambers was the one who had the molds of Ross' face and supplied the noses and the different things that we put on him.

It was just a great job for a young guy. We worked 13, 14, sometimes

The Wild Wild West's *Artemus Gordon (Ross Martin) in three Chase makeups for various Season 4 episodes.*

15 hours a day, and there was a lot of action and activity on the set, a lot of bravado. There was a lot of testosterone goin' on there *[laughs]*. If memory serves, we had to be there by six in the morning, and we'd still be there at seven, eight o'clock at night. I think I was there pretty much all the time. The hairdresser was a woman named Esperanza Corona, who was once Tyrone Power's hairdresser. She was a very elegant Mexican woman and a real pleasure. The hairdressers did men *and* women, and they did wigs and haircuts and all that stuff.

Early on in that fourth season, Ross Martin broke his leg on the set [while shooting "The Night of the Avaricious Actuary"]. While he was being moved to an ambulance on a gurney, I followed along, peeling off his makeup from his face *[laughs]*. Then later in the season, he had a heart attack, so for several episodes he was replaced in the role of Jim

West's partner by a couple of pretty well-known character actors, Charlie Aidman and William Schallert. They were really, really nice guys, and cooperative. That's all you have to do to have the makeup man like you, just be cooperative *[laughs]!* For one episode ["The Night of the Pelican"] I did Aidman as a Chinaman with a bald cap — a pretty elegant makeup. Bald caps were difficult and I loved the challenge of doing them.

I'll tell you one thing that was very funny, but Ross Martin sure didn't think it was funny: He was a little bit of a prima donna, and one of the things that irritated him more than aaanything else, was sitting in the makeup chair for two hours and then, once he was made-up and ready, being kept waiting to do his scenes. There was one regular director, and I don't remember which director it was, who didn't really like Ross very much and, I swear, kept him waiting on purpose *[laughs]*. This director would keep Ross sitting around for *hours*. Actors don't necessarily like having to be *in* that makeup to begin with, and then to have it go on need-lessly used to drive Ross crazy! He didn't mind getting made-up, but he didn't like wasting *his* time waiting. He thought he was a little above that.

Ross was a real old-school actor and he definitely wasn't "one of the boys" [Conrad's crew of regular stuntmen]. *That* was a real collection of characters! They were a terrific bunch of stunt guys who would do *any*thing, because they had this false sense of indestructibility. They were like Conrad's stooges.

Q: What was the atmosphere on the set when a fight or action scene was about to be shot?

Usually there'd be a little excitement in the air, because they weren't the "normal" bunch of people that you'd find on a set; they had that "bravado" thing, and it usually led to some pretty good results.

There was a guy who was Conrad's wardrobe man, Jimmy George, who became Conrad's stunt double because there really *was* a physical like-ness. Jimmy got banged-up on a lot of the stunts he did. In one episode ["The Night of the Diva"] he was supposed to fall from the landing at the top of a staircase and land on his back on a balsa wood table. It was a 15-, 18-foot fall. On his first attempt, he missed the table and landed on his back on the floor. He turned white, and it looked like he was gonna die, but ten minutes later he got up and did it a second time. If he had landed on the table as planned, he would have been all right but this time he clipped the edge of it and hit the floor again. Not one of these guys would ever admit if he was in pain!

Then there was one incident [also on "The Night of the Diva"] where Jimmy had to dive through a breakaway wall that had been made out of stucco. Well, when they had him do it, the stucco hadn't yet dried, so instead of smashing through, he hit this wet stucco with a thud and just barely got through, and fell short of the mark on the other side where he was supposed to land [atop stuntmen waiting to catch him]. *That* knocked him silly too. So Jimmy's stunt career wasn't that long-lived! He was a really nice guy and he was trying so hard. He went back to being a wardrobe man, which is not a terrible job, and finished out his career that way. He was a great guy and everybody liked him.

Well, the stuntmen were *all* the nicest guys. Red West was Elvis Presley's pal; Red had a career working with Elvis, and played parts in lots of Elvis' movies. Then finally he actually became a character actor and got some pretty decent roles. *Very* nice guy. Whitey Hughes was a terrific little guy, Dick Cangey was also a good guy, and Tommy Huff was great too.

Q: You had to come up with different makeups for the stuntmen every week, so that viewers wouldn't realize that they were every villain's henchmen in every episode!

I had to make-up the stuntmen every day; it became a joke! Those stunt guys had to wear every style of mustache and beard. It was just...wild. On that show, there was no stopping: You'd be doing makeup literally all day long. Then after work, there was a cantina across the street called the Backstage which was the scene of a brawl or two. I never got into one there; I came awfully close, but never actually landed a punch. Those kinds of things [after-hours brawls] were not uncommon. When [makeup artist] Frank Griffin and I were doing *The Time Tunnel*, one night at a bar near 20th Century-Fox I saw Frank, a real big, strong, muscular guy, get into a fight with another makeup man, Harry Maret, and they were so drunk they fought for about 20 minutes and neither one of them ever landed a punch *[laughs]!*

Wild Wild West was a great show to work on. I wouldn't want to do it when I was 50, but when I was *that* age, it was fantastic, a wonderful opportunity for a young guy simply because of what I got to do. I went from that onto the *Gunsmoke* series, which was shot on the same lot. That was another real interesting job for a young guy — a lot of sunburns, bruises, beards and scars — but not quite as exciting as *Wild West*. After *Gunsmoke*, I started doing movies. Prosthetic aging and character makeup was really my specialty. For *The Golden Child* [1986] with Eddie Murphy, I created some really bizarre characters. Also memorable for me were *Back to the Future* [1985], *The Stunt Man* [1980] and *The Color Purple* [1985, for which Chase received an Oscar nomination]. My absolute favorite was *Midnight Train to Moscow* [1989] with Billy Crystal, an HBO special filmed in Russia. I did Billy as several characters including a black musi-

Kenneth Chase today.

cian, an old Jewish woman and director Martin Scorsese. [Chase received an Emmy for *Midnight Train to Moscow*.]

In the '60s when I worked on *Wild Wild West*, the movie business and TV was different than it is now. It wasn't so much business, it was a lot of fun. People were light-hearted and knew how to have a good time. Today, working on a TV series is drudgery, it's just not the same. On a given day on *Wild Wild West*, we would do 14, 15 hours worth of work, and yet a group of us on the set intermittently would play Liar's Poker all day long. There were poker games at lunchtime, there were brawls at the Backstage across the street, a lot of kidding-around and a lot of just having a really good time.

Gary Clarke
JOKES'R'US
ON *THE VIRGINIAN*

There was lots of competition for the co-starring role of Steve in Universal's new 90-minute Western series The Virginian *but Clarke prevailed.*

Actor Gary Clarke first came on the movie scene in the late 1950s, strutting his stuff in low-budget j.d. flicks as a prelude to his days of greater success on television. Baby Boomers will remember him as a regular on TV's Michael Shayne *and* Hondo *but his finest hour (and a half) was Universal's* The Virginian *with James Drury, the ambitious 90-minute series set in and around the Wyoming Territory's sprawling Shiloh Ranch. Debuting in 1962,* The Virginian *featured Clarke as cowhand Steve Hill, a young fun-lover rather like Clarke (and* Virginian *co-star Doug McClure) in real life. With* Virginian *seasons now being rounded up for DVD release (with the Timeless Media Group brand), Clarke moseys down the Reminiscence Trail...*

GARY CLARKE: In the early 1960s I was under contract to Universal, I had a seven-year contract, and they were using me in a lot of their TV shows — *Wagon Train, Laramie* and all those. Then we got news of this hour-and-a-half Western that was coming on, *The Virginian,* and *every*body auditioned for it. Once the call goes out [on a new TV series], every agent in town calls any of their clients who are even *close* to the description of a character. It was obvious that *The Virginian* was going to be a big deal: the first hour-and-a-half weekly show sold to a network without a pilot, in color; they were pulling out all the stops, so everybody wanted to audition. Ben Cooper was up for the part of Steve, and one of the producers at Universal was a champion for him. The way it was set up, if you were auditioning for a particular role, no one else who was up for that same role could come on the set. But when it came my turn to audition, I looked up and Ben Cooper was on the set, *with* the producer who was championing him.

Doug McClure and I auditioned together. Doug and I had met already, we'd been kinda social friends, he liked me, I liked him, and for this audition scene, we put together a couple of routines. There was one point during the scene where I jumped up and straddled his waist with my legs, he put his hands under my legs, flipped me up and I did a back flip. I think they liked that. They later shot a scene, kind of a "free-for-all," with 10, 15, 20 actors who were up for the Virginian, Trampas and Steve roles. Jim Drury wasn't there but I know there were guys who were auditioning for the Virginian role; so they had Virginians, Trampases and Steves. This was on an interior set, with all these actors ad-libbing dialogue, etc.; the direction was, "Get out there and do whatever you want." At one point, Ben Cooper pulled his gun on me and I just instinctively put my finger in the barrel *[laughs]*, and I heard them laugh behind camera. And I had made up a song about the Virginian, which I proceeded to sing on-camera. After that was done, it was: "Okay, fellas. Go home and wait."

Jere Henshaw, one of the VIPs there at Universal, was on my side. At a point where we were all still waiting to hear who got what part, he had a party at his house — there were going to be 20, 30 people there. I went to his house and rang the bell, he opened the door and he said, "Oh, hi, Steve. I mean, *Gary*." Huh?? And he said, "No, I didn't say anything. No. No. You didn't hear anything from *me*…!" Then a few days later, I was told that I was Steve! That's how I got it.

Prior to *The Virginian*, I didn't know James Drury at all! Never met Jim. But from the git-go, he was very supportive and fun. Whenever we needed anything, we'd go to Jim — he was that kind of guy. And working with Doug McClure was a hoot. We had the *best* time. It was Jokes'R'Us. We played jokes on the assistant directors, we played jokes on each other, we cut-up in the scenes, we ad-libbed all *over* the place. Most of it was well-received by others…and sometimes, some of it was a pain in the ass to others, I'm sure. We had an assistant director that we loved, a young guy who was fun, and he was always the brunt of our water jokes. One day on the lot, toward the end of the lunch break, it was the a.d.'s job to stand near one particular stage toward the front of the Universal lot and re-gather all of the extras who had broken for lunch and get 'em on a shuttle and get 'em back to the *Virginian* set. Doug and I saw him standing there in the shade of this building, so we filled a huge wastebasket with water and we climbed up the ladder on the side of this 50-foot building. Doug was in front of me on the ladder holding the top of the basket, I was coming up behind him pushing the basket, and we were both climbing one-handed. There had to be ten gallons of water in that basket so how we got up there, I don't know. We got to the roof and we crept over to the edge, and there he was 50 feet down below us. We took this huge basket of water, aimed it and tipped it over. Honest to God, not a drop missed him *[laughs]!*

To get the role, I told 'em I could ride — and I was lying through my teeth. I had once been on a pony, with my mother leading it around a ring, and that was about it. But I figured that from the time that I got the part until we started shooting, I would take horse-riding lessons and I could learn. I was fairly athletic so I didn't perceive that as any kind of a problem. But during the interim between the time I got the part and the start of shooting, it was hectic — getting ready for the show, learning scripts, doing p.r. stuff, and I didn't have time to learn to ride. So *now* I figured that once we started the show, we would do interior stuff first, and while they were doing interior stuff that did not involve me, I could learn how to ride a horse.

Before I continue the horse riding story, I have to tell you about my stuntman. His name was Gary Combs and, prior to *The Virginian*, he had been my double on a couple of *Wagon Trains*. My introduction to Gary was, we were out on a *Wagon Train* set and there was a scene where I was on a horse and it comes running from behind the camera and I jump off and I bulldog this longhorn…or cow…or bull…or what*ever* it was. It was

Gary Clarke got his feet wet movie-wise in horror and youthsploitation flicks from the late 1950s, How to Make a Monster *(1958) with Heather Ames among them.*

an animal with horns *[laughs].* While we were messing around with the scene, an extra said, "Oh, I can bulldog that thing…" and he grabbed this cow by the horns and tried to wrestle him down. Well, the cow kinda just twitched his head — and knocked the guy's front teeth out. *All* of 'em. While he was picking 'em up, along came Gary who must have weighed all of 155 pounds; Gary grabbed this cow and dropped him in a heartbeat.

The first-season cast of The Virginian: *Lee J. Cobb (sitting on rock) as Judge Henry Garth, Roberta Shore as his daughter Betsy and, behind them, Clarke as Steve, James Drury as The Virginian and Doug McClure as Trampas.*

When I got the part of Steve on *The Virginian*, I remembered him and I said I thought he'd be great as my stunt double and I recommended him highly, and they bought it.

So on *The Virginian* I figured that Gary would teach me how to ride. But on the very first day of the very first show, we were out on location, and the first shot was a shot of 50 horses that were going to be herded first by Jim, then by Doug, and then by me. The shot was set up so that the camera would shoot from a moving camera car, *across* the horses to the actor — Jim, then Doug, then me — on his horse. Jim had worked on a dude ranch and he owned horses and he was a good horseman, so he was up first. They said, "Action!," the camera car started, the wranglers whipped up the 20 or 30 horses and they started running. Jim started riding beside them and he was in *among* them and he was going "Hey! Hey!" and whipping the lasso against his chaps…he looked terrific. *I'm* watching this and I'm saying, "Holy [bleep]…!" So I told Gary and his father Del, who was one of the wranglers, "Look, I've practiced mounting, so I'm pretty sure I can get on the horse. And I'm pretty sure…I'm *fairly* sure I can stay on the horse. But I'm a little concerned that I won't be able to stop the horse when it's all excited, galloping with these other horses. I may end up over the Mulholland Hills in the center of Hollywood. Can you do *any*thing for me…?" They started laughing, and they said, "We got a great horse for you. We got Babe." I didn't know who Babe was, but…if she was the horse for me, then God bless her. So they brought out Babe, and I tried a couple of mounts, and that worked.

In the meantime, Jim had finished his shot and they brought all the horses back to the starting point, and now it was Doug's turn. Doug had done rodeo stuff, so he was on his horse with his smile with the 82 teeth all in front, the director yelled "Action!" and they started the horses up, and Doug did the same thing that Jim did but even *better*, he looked great. So I said again to Gary and his father, "If I can't stop my horse, what do I do?" They laughed and they said, "Just aim her toward us, and we'll stop her. Don't worry about it."

They finished with Doug and they were getting all the horses back to the starting point. I asked Gary and his dad, "All right, do you have anything else you want to tell me?" and again they promised me that Babe was a good horse and that I'd be fine. So I walked up to the starting point…one of the wranglers was holding Babe…I took the reins and I jumped up on her. Now, as I was waiting, I leaned over to Babe and I said, "Babe, it's you and me. Be good to me and I'll be good to you. I've got some sugar cubes in the dressing room, okay?" And Babe went *[Clarke sputters like a horse].* So the director yelled "Action!", the camera car went, they whipped up the horses, I jabbed Babe with my spurs, and she was off like a bolt of lightning. And none of this bouncy stuff to get started; she was off at a sprint, and I automatically got into this rhythm. Babe and I *were one.* The horse gods were looking down at me and saying, "Go for it, Gary!" I was riding, I was whipping Babe on both sides of her with my reins, I was going "Yee-haw!" and I took my hat off and Babe was weaving in and out of the other horses — I was doing all of this stuff perfectly, and I could hear the director in the camera car saying [*in an ecstatic voice*], "Oh my God, that's wonderful!" We went for half a mile or something like that, we got to the end of the run, the director said "Cut!" and I aimed Babe toward the wranglers and Gary and Del, who were waiting. And suddenly Babe started stopping and going. Stop and go. Stop and go. Stop and go. Stop and go. The wranglers, laughing, grabbed the reins, and I jumped off. What I was doing wrong, I found out later, was pulling on the reins to get Babe to stop, but also gripping her with my spurs. That'll kinda confuse a horse!

The only other ones who knew I couldn't ride were Jim and Doug. The two of them came over to me, the director came over, and the director said, "Gary, that was fan-*tas*-tic. Jim! Doug! How come *you* couldn't have done it like that?" Jim and Doug rolled their eyes and walked away!

I spent the rest of the day on Babe; any time I wasn't in a scene, Babe and I were out riding. Later in the day, in the afternoon, there was a shot where Jim and Doug and I were to ride fairly fast down a hill and, at the bottom of the hill where the camera was, turn and keep going, and the camera follows us off into the sunset. Jim and Doug were already at the starting point, and as I was riding up, I could see that they were conspiring. But it didn't matter to me because [*in a grand tone of voice] Babe and I were one.* They said "Action" and we came down the hill; Jim and Doug had me on the outside, which would put me closest to the camera as we turned the corner. We raced down and we turned in front of the camera and the camera followed us, and just as we passed the camera, Jim and Doug started edging me off the road. But that was okay, I was doing fine, even off the road. But I looked up, and there was this bush about five feet tall, and I said to myself, "I am dead." Jim and Doug were laughing their asses off. Well, as we approached the bush, Babe leapt into the air…and I kinda leaned forward, so I wouldn't slide off…Babe cleared the bush like an Olympic horse and landed on her forefeet, and I leaned back. Perfect! The director said, "That was *great*, we'll find a way to leave that in! Jim! Doug! You ought to take lessons from Gary!" And that was my first day on the show.

Every other episode, maybe, we would leave the Universal lot and shoot out on location, but there were plenty of places on the lot that looked like they were out in the country. But on the Universal lot we always had to be careful, because in the distance we could hear the Hollywood Freeway in the background. When we did go on location, usually we would be out at a place called Albertson's Ranch. There were rolling hills, and Red

Clarke with Roberta Shore, a regular on The Virginian *its first three seasons. Clarke lasted just one season, but made a few returns in Season 3.*

Rock Canyon was out there where they did a lot of the *old* Westerns. But finally they had to stop shooting there because there were too many cars and too many wires and stuff like that.

As for Lee J. Cobb [the series regular playing ranch owner Judge Garth]...I'm working with him on *The Virginian* for, oh, I don't know, a couple of months and, man, just to be able to work with this guy...! It gets so that when I'm around him, I'm tongue-tied. So after a few months, I decide that I should have a little conversation with him — I was still tongue-tied, and *maybe* there was *some*thing he would say that would help. So we're riding out to the location, Jim Drury's in the front seat, Doug McClure is in the middle in the back seat, Lee is on the right and I'm on the left, and Jim and Doug know that I want to talk to Lee about something. So we get to the location, they get out, the driver gets out and I'm there with Lee, who's just lit up his ever-present cigar. He's just kind of relaxing, staring straight ahead. I said, "Lee, this...uh...I don't mean to...I just thought...thought *maybe* you might be able to shed a little light...but maybe this has happened to you before but I...uh...uh...uh...I've noticed that when I, I, I'm around you that I'm tongue-tied. I just...you know, I just admire your work as an actor and here we've been working for months and I find that I'm around you and I can't *talk*. And I just thought maybe there would be something that you could...*[nervous laugh]*...that you could *say* that would help...would help..."

He takes a long draw on the cigar...lets the smoke curl out...doesn't say anything. I wait for what seemed like two days and he doesn't say anything. I say, "Look, I don't want to intrude on your morning, Lee, but this is just something that has been kind of *eating* at me," and I stammer it all out a second time. Another draw on the cigar. More smoke curling out. Doesn't even look my way. And I'm watching him. I say, "Well, obviously this isn't a good time to talk. And you can go to Hell and kiss my butt for all I care!" I get out of the car, slam the door. I'm pissed off. And, ironically, virtually all my scenes that day are with Lee *[laughs]*!

So we're doing these scenes, and for me they're going well because I don't *give* a damn. I'm thinking, "Hey, Lee. Hey, big shot. Who *gives* a damn?" We're doing the scenes, and the director Virgil Vogel comes up to me at one point and he says, "I don't know what you're doin', Gary, but keep it up, it's *great*." The second-to-last scene of the day, or something like that, Lee's in his chair and he's again smoking his cigar and I'm pacing back and forth waiting for the cameras to get set up. Back and forth like a pacing lion. And I glance over at him a couple times and I catch this little glint in his eyes, this little gleam. It hit me like a ton of bricks — like the butt of a pistol on my forehead. I look at him and I say, "You son of a bitch — you did that on purpose. *You did it on purpose!*" And he laughs…stands up…picks me up…hugs me…and that was *it*. Imagine Lee J. Cobb going that far to help a fellow actor get past a little block. 'Cause, I mean, it took guts to do what he did; he didn't know how violent I was, or *could* have been. (Well, I *wasn't*, and he probably knew that.) So after that, I just *adored* the man.

In a lot of the shows, I was the comedic relief, but fortunately I also got to do some "heavier" stuff. One episode, "Duel at Shiloh" [a semi-remake of the 1955 movie *Man Without a Star*], depicted in flashbacks the first time I came to the ranch. The story started with me stowing away on a freight train, and a brakeman [actor-stuntman John Day] finds me and stops the train in the middle of nowhere and tells me to start walkin'. We have a fight, the brakeman knocks me out and I roll onto the tracks. Brian Keith was the guest star in that episode, playing Johnny, another guy ridin' the rails. Johnny pulls me off the tracks just as the train is starting to move again, saves my life, throws me in the freight car with him, and we become friends. Later in the episode he teaches me how to shoot, and in the script all it said was, "Johnny teaches Steve how to shoot." So Brian Keith and I made up the whole scene, we devised everything that went on in it. It was hysterical. I almost shoot off my foot; I try spinning my gun and it ends up in my holster butt-first; things like that.

At one point in the scene, I inadvertently fire the gun in his direction while he's setting up cans to shoot, and he walks up to me and pounded his fist on my chest. I was just a gnat's eyebrow away from hitting him back, because he *really* gave me a shot. But I didn't, because I'm an actor and I'm "in character," and Steve would *not* have hit him back. That episode, I found out some time later, was the one that the *Virginian* producers would show new directors: "This is the kind of thing that we want, this is the style that we want."

Some of our other guest stars included George C. Scott; in that episode ["The Brazen Bell"] there was a scene where I taught *him* how to shoot, and after the scene he said [*Clarke imitates Scott's low-key voice*], "Very well done, Gary…that was very well done…thank you…" Whoa! Robert Redford; I remember just sitting down with him and having a regular conversation. I liked him, he was great to work with. We also had Fabian, and he was fun. I kept telling him that his eyes looked too big. He asked [*stammering*], "What do you mean? What do you mean?" I said, "Stop opening your eyes so much. You look like you're in constant surprise!" Lee Marvin was bigger than life, and funny and professional. Charlie Bronson, Bette Davis…I could go on and on.

Q: Co-starring on The Virginian — *was that the point in your career when you started getting recognized on the street?*

Yes. Right away. I liked it. I *expected* it. That's the point when girls ask *you* for dates. But you know that they're not asking *you*, they're asking the character that you play! This is a story you probably won't be able to use, but I'm gonna tell you anyway. I had this alpaca sweater that I really liked. It was orange, kinda blousy, but it had tight cuffs and a tight waist. I lent it to my younger brother, who was in high school at the time, 15 or 16, and *he* lent it to a friend of his because the friend was going to England. And while he was there, he met several English young ladies, and he would talk about his best friend has a brother who was in television. "Oh really? On what show?" "*The Virginian.*" "*The Virginian*?! Well, who *is* it?" "Gary Clarke." "Gary Clarke?!" "Yes. In fact, this is his sweater." And on occasion, he…I think the phrase is "got lucky" *[laughs]*…and he took a girl to bed. *But* she would not let him have sex *unless* he was wearing Gary Clarke's sweater *[laughs]!*

So, yes, that was the point at which I started getting a lot of fan mail, and people stopping me on the street: "Say, aren't you…?" Once, somebody came up and said, "Oh! You're…ummm…I watch your show all the time, I love it. Tell me…what's it like to work with Hoss?"

Q: Did you think you got your fair share of episodes devoted to your character?

Oh, you never do. You always want *more*. That may have been part of the reason that I wasn't brought back for another season. I did something that was stupid: I went over the head of the producer, Frank Price, and went to see Lew Wasserman, the head of the studio, the big shot. I figured I could do that, because my agent was married to his daughter. I walked in, and it was like *[in an awed whisper]*, "Ooooooo…the inner sanctum!" I was in the big black building, the top floor, sitting down with God [Wasserman]. And God offered me a Coke, and I took it. And we talked, and I said, "I was just wondering if maybe I might be able to get a couple more shows during the season…?" — I don't remember exactly what I said, but it was probably arrogant and stupid. Then we went into hiatus, and during the hiatus I got a call from my agent and he said, "Gary, Universal didn't pick you up." "*What*??" *But* — strangely enough, they brought me back for three more episodes ["Felicity's Spring," "Big Image…Little Man" and "The Girl from Yesterday," all Season Three], I came back as the same character, and they must have paid me three or four times what I was getting as a regular on the show. Which wasn't bad!

I have the new *Virginian* DVD set, and I've watched *[pause]*...a couple. I watched "Duel at Shiloh" and "Roar from the Mountain" with Jack Klugman. I think that's it. Jim, Roberta Shore, Randy Boone and I have done a couple of film festivals together and we always have a big box of those DVDs that we can sell, so we can make a few bucks off that. I did one [the 10th Annual Saddle Up festival] in Pigeon Forge, Ten-

nessee, earlier this year [2010] and I got to take my daughter Ava with me. She's 16 now and just gorgeous, and talented. I have to tell you about her: When she was eight years old, Ava and I did the Abbott & Costello "Who's on First?" routine during a talent show at our church. I thought there'd be maybe a hundred people there...and then we got there, and there were a *thousand* people. Well, I figured she was going to panic. Our routine started with me [playing Abbott's character] talking from the stage to the audience, telling them, "We're starting a baseball team, and I want a lot of you to volunteer to be on it." And from

Clarke and, of all people, Broncho Billy Anderson, the first Western film star — beginning with The Great Train Robbery *(1903)!*

the back of the room came: "Heyyyyyyy, Dad-deeee!" [instead of "Hey, Abbott!"]. We were the first act in the show so there were still people in the aisle, and Ava was supposed to run up the aisle and come up on stage — and I didn't know if she could *do* it, with all the people in the way. Well, she ran around the people, she dodged them, she ran up on stage, and she was phenomenal. Twice — *twice* — she corrected me on stage *[laughs]*. Up to that point, whenever we did anything like that, it had been: "And now I present Gary Clarke and his daughter," but from that day on, it was "And now I present Ava Clarke and...what's-his-name." *[laughs]* She was a hoot! So in Pigeon Forge we did "Who's on First?" again, and they loved it. And again, what started as "It's Gary Clarke from *The Virginian* and his daughter" quickly became "It's Ava and what's-his-name from *The Virginian*." I am *doomed*, Tom, I am *doomed!*

Robert Clarke
ON THE RKO RANGE

Playing cowboys-and-Indians as a kid didn't prepare actor Robert Clarke for the horse-riding action required of him in some of his RKO Westerns. He's seen here in 1950's Riders of the Range.

In the beginning days of his long Hollywood career, Robert Clarke learned the movie-acting ropes at RKO, playing supporting parts in dozens of A- and B-pictures. Some of the young contract player's best early opportunities came via the company's Westerns, made on the studio lot and on location at scenic spots like Lone Pine. Here he recalls their stars James Warren and Tim Holt, the leading ladies, fellow supporting players (including Raymond Burr), and his first, harrowing horseback chase scene.

ROBERT CLARKE: I've always had a fondness for Westerns, partly because I enjoyed them as a kid in Oklahoma, and also partly because it was the RKO B Westerns that provided me with some of my first decent-sized screen roles. Some of my earliest memories of growing up in Oklahoma City are of playing cowboys and Indians with the other kids in the neighborhood. Our role models were such known names as Tom Mix, Buck Jones and Hoot Gibson. I recall my dad taking me to a Saturday matinee in which Hoot Gibson rescued the leading lady from a runaway horse by lassoing her and quickly tossing his lariat over the limb of a tree, then pulling her up as the horse sped on past. The next anxious moments saw Hoot and the girl seesawing from the ground up to the top of the tree and back down until finally they both ended up on the ground. I couldn't wait to get home and try the trick with my little brother. But the rope broke, and he came tumbling down on top of me.

Throughout my career I've appeared opposite several of *the* most famous cowboy stars: Tim Holt at RKO, Guy (Wild Bill Hickok) Madison, Clayton (The Lone Ranger) Moore and others on TV, John Wayne (although not in a Western) and more. I've also worked with some very unusual and *unlikely* cowboy heroes, like bandleader Harry James. But the first several Westerns in which I worked starred what you'd have to call a forgotten Western actor, James Warren.

In the late 1930s and early '40s, before I came on the scene at RKO, their top B Western star was Tim Holt, son of the actor Jack Holt. Tim made his first film appearances in some of his famous father's silents, and by 1940 he had risen from bits and supporting parts to being the star of his own low-budget Western series at RKO. In 1943, at the height of World War II, Tim was inducted into the military. His father was also in the service at the same time, and in fact rose to the rank of major.

In Tim's absence, RKO initiated a series of B Westerns based on novels by Zane Grey. The first two, *Nevada* [1944] and *West of the Pecos* [1945], starred Robert Mitchum, who was at the beginning of what would turn out to be a very long and distinguished film career. The producer of these

Westerns was a fellow named Herman Schlom, and the story went around that Herman suggested to Bob Mitchum that he change his name to Mitch*ell*. Mitchum asked, "Well, why?," and Herman said, "'Mitchum' — it doesn't look so good on the screen." To which Mitchum replied, "Well, *your* name's on the screen, and your name is *Schlom*."

Needless to say, Mitchum wouldn't change his name, much to his credit. Even in those early days when Mitchum was busy in these low-budget cowboy pictures, the people working with him could tell that he was headed onward and upward. Mitchum's performance in MGM's *Thirty Seconds Over Tokyo* [1944] impressed a producer named Sid Rogell, and Sid signed Mitchum to a long-term RKO contract. With Tim Holt in the service, RKO put Mitchum into some of these little Zane Grey Westerns, and the next thing you knew, his career was off and running.

After Mitchum's two Zane Greys, the reins were handed over to James Warren, who starred in three, *Wanderer of the Wasteland* [1945], *Sunset Pass* [1946] and *Code of the West* [1947]. I also acted in all three of those, playing either the renegade son of some rancher, or the undisciplined brother of some pretty cowgirl. I enjoyed doing them. The parts were substantial and they actually called for some acting; being placed in dramatic situations gave me an opportunity to *act*, which was what I wanted to do. The other roles that RKO handed me were often so limited, some of them so *small*, that the Westerns seemed to offer me many more opportunities.

Jim Warren had been under contract at MGM before he came over to RKO. He was a very agreeable, easygoing kind of a fellow; he was tall and slender — almost Gary Cooper-ish — and he had the look of a Western type. My first picture with him was *Wanderer of the Wasteland*, based on a Zane Grey novel that had previously been filmed by Paramount in 1935. Warren played a character who had been orphaned as a child when his dad was slain on the Mojave Desert. He was taken in by a middle-aged couple and grew up with *their* young son. Now adults, Jim and his life-long friend Chito Rafferty (Richard Martin) find a clue to the killer's identity which leads them to the ranch of Robert Barrat. Warren admires Barrat and accepts the job of keeping Barrat's disreputable young nephew Jay (myself) away from the gambling tables in the local saloon. Warren also falls in love with Jay's sister (Audrey Long), but avoids her because he fears that her uncle may turn out to be his father's killer.

Chito Rafferty, the slow-witted, girl-crazy Mexican-Irish sidekick, was played by Richard Martin, a prince of a guy and one of my best friends. Dick was the type who would do you a favor and, if you tried to thank him, tell you, "Well, that's what friends are for." I saw Dick my first day on

A contract player doing uncredited bits in many RKO movies, Clarke got his best early roles in the studio's Westerns.

the RKO lot, and I recall thinking that he was about as handsome a guy as you could find. Dick was standing in the doorway of the casting office and I said hello and introduced myself, and we had a brief conversation. I was so impressed with the looks of the guy that I felt sure that he was headed for stardom. And he *was*, in a manner of speaking; Chito became Tim Holt's sidekick in Westerns once Tim got out of the service, and Dick stayed with that series right up into the 1950s. (Dick had grown up in West Hollywood where he had a lot of friends who were Hispanic, and he found he could do a very good Spanish or Mexican accent.) But Dick didn't reach the Robert Taylor or Tyrone Power pinnacle that I thought he might have achieved. He once said that he never really felt that he had the acting qualities or charisma that goes with being a superstar. He never quite felt comfortable playing himself and so he enjoyed playing Chito. Of course, if that part was cast today, they would hire a Hispanic person, not Anglo-American, because the Screen Actors Guild now is pressed to give opportunities to those of different ethnic backgrounds. But Dick did get the chance to play Chito, and he found that he could work behind that accent and feel comfortable.

Another thing I recall distinctly about *Wanderer of the Wasteland* is how surprised I was at the first daily rushes. I saw them and I thought to myself, "Is that *me*?" I heard the voice and *it* sounded familiar, and then I looked at myself and thought, "Gee, I didn't know I looked like that." (I don't know *what* I expected.) I was quite young then, 25 approximately, and I looked even younger than *that*, and I was kind of taken aback.

In the second James Warren Western, *Sunset Pass*, he was an express company agent who sets out with Chito (this time played by John Laurenz) to stop a series of Arizona train robberies. On a train they meet Nan Leslie, returning home to her family's ranch, and Jane Greer, an entertainer. Bandits hold up the train, and evidence points to my character Ash (Nan's brother — of course) as one of the robbers.

I'm sometimes asked if I was ever asked to do things that were beyond my capabilities in Westerns or in some of the other action-type pictures I was in. The truth is that they generally had stuntmen on hand to double the actors in any sort of dangerous situation, because an injured actor can throw an entire production behind schedule. I did like doing my own stunts whenever I was permitted, because I'd heard that some of the biggest stars, Douglas Fairbanks for instance, were renowned for doing that. (It wasn't until years later that I found out that even Fairbanks and other stars like him did have stuntmen for some of their hairier stunts, regardless of *what* they said.)

It was on one of the James Warren pictures that I was in my first Western chase scene. I had done some riding back in Oklahoma, where we used to get a horse rental for 50 cents an hour when I was a kid, and so I wasn't unfamiliar with horses, but I was *not* what you'd call an experienced horseman. However, I wanted RKO to *think* I was. The scene called for me to ride my horse behind the camera car and fire my gun, supposedly at whoever it was I was chasing. (This was in the Alabama Hills, just outside of Lone Pine.) What I realized once we started was that I also had to keep my hat from blowing off. With your left hand handling the reins and the right hand firing the .45, that's not always so easy. (Once or twice, the hat *would* blow off and we'd have to go back and start again.) And then, of course, you were firing right over the horse's head, near his right ear, which the horse didn't like. There were three different sizes of blank cartridge (the full load, the half-load and a quarter-load), and the full load really was a loud bang.

The horse I was riding evidently had a problem with his front hooves, because as he ran, he kept clicking them together. So not only was he stumbling, but every time I'd fire the gun, it would scare him a little bit. The camera car was going 35 or 40 miles an hour and I had to keep up with it; the men in the car were waving me on, "Come closer — closer," and the driver was watching me in his rear view mirror. Well, this was a first for me, needless to say. With every shot of the gun, the horse would bow its neck and veer to the right, to get its ears away from the noise. By the side of the road was a drainage ditch, and every time I fired the gun, the horse got closer to the edge of it. To make a long story short, I got through the scene in one piece: I didn't get thrown, and we didn't go into the ditch, but I sure did have trouble staying aboard, and I don't mind admitting that I was glad when *that* particular ride was over. After the first one or two Westerns, it got to be easier, of course, and I became more adept in riding with a posse and that sort of thing. I also realized that most horses were well-trained for use in movies — sometimes better-trained than the actor.

The last of the James Warrens was *Code of the West*, in which I had less than usual to do. I was once again the brother of the leading lady (Debra Alden), and this time Jim and John Laurenz (as Chito) clean up a gang terrorizing the Arizona strip. It was on *Code of the West* that I had my first opportunity to observe Raymond Burr in action. He had just come out from New York, and this was one of his first experiences in front of a camera. Ray and I had a dialogue scene together, and after I'd done my dialogue with the camera on me, the camera switched around to Ray's closeup and I stood alongside the camera to give Ray *his* cues. Ray was so nervous, he began to perspire like you wouldn't believe. Of course, later he became very confident as an actor and so expert at the parts he played in movies and on TV, Perry Mason and Ironside and so on. But in that little part in *Code of the West*, he was extremely nervous, fighting to get the words out, and the perspiration just poured out of him. The makeup man was there with a sponge, trying to keep him dry, and we had two or three takes before he finally got it. It's amazing the way actors can change and grow, from modest beginnings and a stage fright attitude; once they get going, they suddenly sprout and blossom and they've got the world in the palm of their hand. That was certainly the case with Raymond Burr.

Tim Holt got his discharge in late 1945, but instead of returning to RKO, he first played one of the Earps in director John Ford's *My Darling Clementine* [1946] with Henry Fonda and Victor Mature. After that he came back to RKO, replacing James Warren as star of the Zane Grey series. I was in four of Tim's B Westerns, two while I was under contract to RKO and then two more after I had begun freelancing. I know from reading about Tim and from meeting some of his fans that my first film with Tim, *Thunder Mountain* [1947], has the reputation of being one of his best. In the movie, Tim returns to his Grass Valley homestead after agricultural college to learn that an old family feud between Tim's clan and the Jorth family is still going strong. Steve Brodie and I played the Jorth brothers and Martha Hyer played our sister. The real villains keeping the feud alive are a pair of sidewinders (Harry Woods and Tom Keene) and a crooked sheriff (Harry Harvey) who have gotten advance word that an irrigation company intends to build a dam on the Holt land, making it the most valuable ranch in Arizona.

The gals who worked in these Tim Holt Westerns enjoyed them for some of the same reasons that I did, not the least of which was the fact that they were a start in the business. Jane Greer, who was also in *Sunset Pass*, was a pretty sophisticated gal (and a good actress, as she later proved), but I got the impression that she didn't care too much about being in the thing. She was a bit blasé about it, to put it frankly, but she was *funny* — she had a great sense of humor. It was a job, she was a contract player and she did what she had to do or RKO would put her on suspension and lay-off.

But Martha Hyer, who was in *Thunder Mountain*, was quite an ambitious actress even then, and she seemed to be more into putting her career ahead of everything else. And I mean *everything* else. She didn't have a car then, so I picked her up in my second-hand Ford to go to the bus the morning we were leaving for Lone Pine. (She had a rented room in a nice neighborhood not far from RKO.) As she got in my car, she said, "Oh, my teeth are *killing* me." I asked, "What's the matter?" and she said, "I just had all my four front teeth capped *yesterday*." She was in so much pain, but it meant so much to her to look her best that she'd gone through this *very* painful procedure. Nobody does that all at once, but *she* did, in order to be ready for the picture. I remember too that she was very aware

Another regular in RKO's B-Westerns of the 1940s was Harry Woods, seen with Clarke in three James Warrens and one Tim Holt. This shot is from one of the Warrens, Sunset Pass.

of her weight and felt that she had a weight problem, and she was trying desperately to reduce. She later got it completely under control, after which she got into bigger pictures and better parts. Like Jane Greer and Barbara Hale and other contract actresses at RKO, Martha later enjoyed quite a career.

Steve Brodie was also ambitious. Steve was a Kansan who'd gotten into the picture business after working in stock, and he certainly didn't seem to lack any self-esteem. I remember that on one of the Westerns (we were in several together) he was practicing the fast mount of his horse. He wanted to be able to run and hit that stirrup and get on the horse in one leap, rather than run and stop and step up. Some of the stunt guys were very good about helping him, and the director, whoever it was on that particular picture, told him that if he missed the stirrup, they'd let him do it again. Steve was trying to make things look professional and to make his own character look good, and always seemed to have things pretty much under control. He liked to laugh a lot, and he was always joking off-screen.

Tim Holt wasn't that way at all. I found Tim to be a very serious person as well as a very serious actor. He was a quick study who always came to the set prepared, always knew his lines, and could handle a gun or a horse as well as any other actor working in pictures. He never said or did anything to make you aware that *he* was the star, that his was the name in big capital letters above the title while yours was the one in smaller letters below. He also never felt that he had to be "on" between takes; Tim wasn't into entertaining the crew. Many actors feel that they've got to be as good between sequences, and they *use* and *lose* a lot of the energy that they should have saved for the camera. Tim behaved as though he was part of the production office: He knew that this was a business and he'd do everything he could to keep the pictures on schedule. The other thing I recall about Tim was that he really came across as though he could have been a real-life cowboy. I read not too long ago that, even when he was in military school, Tim expressed a desire to be a cowboy star, and years later he achieved it. His acting career could have gone in another, more dramatic direction, as one can see from his performances in movies like *The Magnificent Ambersons* [1942], but he chose to stick with his Western motif.

Thunder Mountain was a good comeback picture for Tim as he returned to his old RKO stamping grounds. Lone Pine was no Monument Valley, but it was rugged country, highly photogenic, and it gave the movie some wonderful atmosphere and the same look as a much bigger budgeted

Clarke took aim at becoming a Hollywood star, but generally had to settle for leading roles in B- (and Z-) pictures, smaller parts in bigger pictures, and lots of TV work. For more about his life and career, check out his 1996 autobiography To "B" or Not to "B" — A Film Actor's Odyssey.

Western. *Thunder Mountain* also featured plenty of action and even a few laughs courtesy of Dick Martin, who returned (for good) in the role of Chito.

I had a much smaller part in *Under the Tonto Rim* [1947], my second picture with Tim. In this one, he was the owner of a stage line whose best friend, one of his drivers, is killed by a gang of outlaws who swoop down on the stagecoach to kidnap a girl (Nan Leslie). Tim devotes himself to tracking the killers, who are known as the Tonto Rim Gang. This was another well-done Western that looked like a more ambitious picture than it actually was because the director Lew Landers and his cameraman got the most out of the Lone Pine locations. Playing a small part as a sheriff's deputy was another RKO stock player, a handsome son of a gun named Lex Barker. I didn't get to know him too well at the time, but I saw him again several years later in New York, after he'd gotten the part of Tarzan, and we chatted for a few minutes about old times. He said, "Boy, you think it's tough acting when you first start out as a Western actor, learning how to use guns and all. Try acting without any *clothes*." He told me that when he played Tarzan, he never knew where to put his hands. He had no pockets, he didn't have anything except that loincloth.

I've been asked if there was any sort of family feeling or sense of camaraderie making these Tim Holt Westerns, which often had the same casts, the same assistant directors, the same prop guys and so on. We did have a nice camaraderie when we'd be up at Lone Pine. We'd spend three, four, five days, perhaps a week, up there whenever we'd make a picture. One of the things I remember best about Lone Pine is how terribly, terribly hot it could get in the summer. But, as unbearable as it was in the heat of the day, at night it was cool and beautiful. In the evenings we would have dinner and sit around the lobby of the Dow Hotel, or sometimes take a walk, just for something to do. At night there wasn't much *to* do in Lone Pine: There was a local saloon or two, but I didn't join in the fun there — I wasn't much for the booze. I think there was one movie theater in Lone Pine, and of course no television. When we'd go up to Lone Pine, RKO would save money by putting two actors in the same hotel room. I roomed with Jason Robards Sr., who had been a star on the stage in New York years before. Until he told me about it, I was unaware of the career he'd had in the theater. He mentioned that one of the long-running plays he did in New York was called *Lightnin'*, and that after *Lightnin'* he came to California to work in films. By the time Jason and I were doing these Westerns together, he was a man in his 50s, now a contract player (a character man) at RKO.

I came back to RKO as a freelancer for the other two Holt Westerns, *Riders of the Range* [1950] and *Pistol Harvest* [1951], RKO didn't exercise my option in the summer of 1947, so I left the studio and went to New York to work in summer stock. When I came back from New York, I went over to the RKO casting office to see Dick Stockton and Eddie Rhine. I told them about the work I'd done back East, including a Broadway play, and they asked me if I'd be interested in doing a Tim Holt Western. They told me that it was a very good part, running the length of the picture, and they said they'd up my pay a little (I got $500 a week instead of $400).

I went for it, but what Dick and Eddie didn't know was that (by offering me this Western) they were reinforcing the feelings of doubt I was having about my career. Here I was, coming back from New York and a Broadway play, and the first job I got was right back in a Tim Holt Western. "What have I *done*?" I asked myself. "Have I made the wrong choice of professions here?" To get back to California from New York, I had hitched a ride with a songwriter, an older guy who wanted somebody to share the cost of the gas. We had come through Oklahoma, where we stopped for a few hours and I visited two or three friends who had become quite successful in business. It seemed like they were making it real big, and now here I was back in Hollywood and, in effect, starting from scratch by agreeing to do this B Western.

By this point, Tim's Westerns were no longer based on Zane Grey's novels (not that they really ever were). In *Riders of the Range*, I was back to playing the troublesome brother, this time opposite Jacqueline White. The villain in this one was played by Tom Tyler, who (like Tom Keene) wore the white hat in Westerns for years and then, when he got older, started wearing the black one. The movie also featured the wonderful Robert Barrat, who was in several of these Holt pictures with me. Not only was he a very nice man, he was also a really good, stalwart character actor. He was born in New York City and had worked on Broadway before he went into the picture business. He told me interesting stories about his career; I recall Barrat talking about acting opposite Edward G. Robinson at Warners, and how dominant and selfish Robinson was to work with. Barrat said Robinson "wanted it all," he wanted to be the center of everything, and he didn't want to give any of the spotlight to any of the other actors. Ida Lupino later expressed the same kind of attitude about Robinson, so apparently Robinson didn't have too many people who liked him — not actors, anyway.

By the time of *Riders of the Range*, RKO was starting to cut corners a little bit on these B Westerns. (At this point, you could see Westerns on

TV for free, so I guess it didn't make much economic sense for the studios to put as much effort into their B Westerns as they once did.) The director of *Riders of the Range*, Lesley Selander, was very adept at what he did, one of the best illustrations I can give of a fast Western director. By the time we actors would finish shooting a scene, Les was already walking away; from 15 or 20 feet away, he'd hear it finish, look around and say, "Okay,

Clarke dining out with two lucky fans in 1997. He died at age 85 in 2005.

cut." And Les would already be halfway to the next place where we had to shoot. The crew would have to *run* to keep up with Les. That was what Les was famous for: He was off and running to the next setup before the crew had broken down the last one.

My final picture with Tim Holt was *Pistol Harvest*. Tim had played different characters (always with the same amigo, Chito) in the earlier pictures, but now he was playing "Tim Holt" in his Westerns the way Roy Rogers played "himself" in his. He was a ranch foreman in *Pistol Harvest* and Robert Wilke and I played a couple of saddle tramps hired by a crooked banker (Mauritz Hugo) to ambush Tim and Chito. Bob Wilke was the lead heavy and I was the kid outlaw because we were physically two different types. Bob had that great, mean face that made him a good actor to have in Westerns. A year or so later, he played one of the badmen in *High Noon* [1952] with Gary Cooper and that was the beginning of better days for Bob. After *High Noon*, his price went way up and he played good supporting roles in lots of top Westerns.

By the early 1950s, the B Western was nearing the end of the trail, done in by TV. The RKO B Westerns weren't art but for people like me, Barbara Hale, Lex Barker, Steve Brodie, Jane Greer, Dick Martin and a lot of others, they provided a great opportunity to get our feet wet in the picture business. I was delighted to be cast in them: We were kids, having fun making movies. Our hopes and dreams were up in the stars, and for some of us, many of them never came true. But it sure was fun to *dream*.

Robert Colbert

MAVERICK DAYS

Jack Kelly, Roger Moore and Robert Colbert as Bart, Beauregard and Brent on TV's hit Western Maverick. *Colbert wanted the Brent role like St. Patrick wanted more snakes.*

The Warner Brothers movie factory went into hyperdrive in the mid-1950s when it moved whole-hog into TV production: One series after another after another was created and shot on the Burbank lot, many of them action-oriented, and a large number of young actors and actresses went from obscurity to national exposure by joining their starring casts. Among them was handsome Robert Colbert, a Long Beach native who signed on Warners' dotted line and, before the veritable ink was dry, found himself on the soundstages of Colt .45, Sugarfoot, Cheyenne, Lawman, Bronco *and more. There was even a short, unexpected and* unwanted *stint as yet another Maverick brother on the most popular series in Warners' Western lineup,* Maverick.

ROBERT COLBERT: I grew up in the Ojai Valley, and a plateau up on the mountain above us was a meadow filled with wild horses. I would go up and jump on the back of one of those things and ride him all over that meadow, with no rope or *anything*. These horses would run under tree branches tryin' to get me off *[laughs]*, they did every-damn-thing they could, and, boy, did I learn how to ride a horse! Then when my [TV-movie acting career] came along, one of the first things I did was a Mustang commercial for Ford. There were 27 guys on horseback, in Civil War uniforms, and I led them on a charge where I came over a bluff and we slid down the side of a hill made of shale. I brought the horse's head up and he slid to the bottom of this hill on his ass, with 20-something guys behind me, all of them with drawn sabers! We hit the bottom of this hillside, whoever was left *[laughs]*, and we raced across this field and came side by side with a guy driving a pretty girl down the road in a Mustang convertible. So I was no master, but I had a *pretty* good training with horses.

Westerns were *all* the glory in those days. We had about eight of 'em at Warner Brothers alone, *Cheyenne, Maverick, Bronco*, you name it. Westerns, Westerns, Westerns! The Hudkins brothers were all over the place, teaching people how to drive stagecoaches and everything *else* you could think of. Here I had all these great guys guiding me through this stuff, and so I was doing trooper mounts, which is where you run up to the rear of the horse and you jump up in the air and put your hands on his rump, you catapult yourself on up into the saddle, and then the horse takes off at a full gallop from that moment. I would do things like that, the Pony Express mount and so on. I would do all those, it was nothing, and I just had fun. You couldn't *buy* a vacation like any one of the Western shows I did. Just bein' out there in the wide open spaces with great guys and horses and beautiful women and good food…and then you got *paid* for it. Not much, but you got paid! A fellow named Tony Aquila would make all the saddles and he would make up holsters, any color, any design that you could dream of. He'd make you a quick-draw holster, whether you wanted to draw with your arm across your belly to protect your guts while you were reaching for your gun, or if you wanted to have double-holsters with speed releases, if you wanted swivel holsters, if you wanted

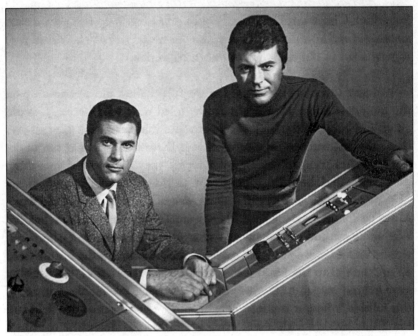

Colbert fared better in sci-fi than in Westerns, top-lining the Irwin Allen series The Time Tunnel *with James Darren in the 1966-67 season.*

hard leather, smooth leather, if you wanted rawhide, *anything*. And there would be quick-draw contests all the time. We'd have blanks and the whole bit if we wanted *[laughs]* — that only happened on rare occasions.

But when it came to quick-draw, everybody thought he was Tom Mix, for Christ's sake. Peter Brown was very good. He studied along with Sammy Davis, Jr., who loved coming over to Warner Brothers and hanging out on the Western sets. Sammy was a cowboy *nut*, and he brought a bunch of holsters, and he got pretty darn good as I understand it. *Every-body* was good by *my* standards; there were some that were outstanding, but none of 'em were actors, they would be the Hudkins brothers. One great guy was the stuntman who doubled Charlton Heston in the *Ben-Hur* [1959] chariot race, Joe Canutt. I knew the guy very well, I hung out with him, he was in my home many times. This guy used to throw on 90 pounds of strap-on weights and run out the back door of Warner Brothers and run straight up the mountain, a damn mountain I couldn't have *climbed* by myself with a cane and somebody pullin' me on a rope! I haaaated him *[laughs]!* No, we all loved him and respected what he did.

Just about every *week* I was in a different Warners show, workin' con-

stantly, working amongst all these stars and just havin' the time of my life over there. Even when there was a strike by the writers, why, Warners gave birth to a guy named "W. Hermanos," which was Warner Brothers in Spanish, and "he" wrote a lot of scripts. What Warners would do is, they would take the script for an episode of, say, *Bronco*, something that had already been shot and shown, and they'd eradicate *Bronco* on the title page and type over it *Cheyenne*. And then they'd replace, throughout the script, the names of the *Bronco* characters with the names of the *Cheyenne* characters. They would even take a Western script, again say *Bronco*, and make it a *Bourbon Street Beat*, a modern-day deal. And now, instead of jumpin' on a horse, you'd be climbin' into a taxi! All of a sudden we were redoing old scripts that were all written long before the writers' strike, and we just kept workin' as if there was no strike at *all*. I always wanted to change my name to W. Hermanos and go down to the Guild and collect all those residuals that that puppy must have made *[laughs]*. There must have been millions waitin' for this dude down there, that nobody ever got!

I was up for a film called *Black Gold* [1963], a story about the oil fields and roughnecks on the order of that old Clark Gable-Spencer Tracy film *Boom Town* [1940]. I was really looking to a chance to have that film, and I felt I pretty much had that in the bag. One day I was sent down to wardrobe and I thought I was going down there for a wardrobe test for *Black Gold*. They started putting me into this cowboy outfit, and it wasn't until the jacket went on that I realized it was *Maverick*. I didn't come out lookin' like Clark Gable, I came out lookin' like Jim Garner [star of *Maverick*]! This was at the time when Jim was fighting with Jack Warner because Jim wanted more money and they wouldn't give it to him, so he walked. That pissed Jack off, he and Jim ended up in a blood feud, and Jim was blackballed in this town for about two years, they wouldn't let him work. So now, as I was walking down the main street of Warner Brothers on my way to a screen test or something, everybody was hangin' out of the windows and lookin', they thought Jim Garner was back on the lot *[laughs]!* Turns out they wanted to put me on *Maverick* as a new Maverick brother, a younger brother named Brent. When I found that out, I said, "Jesus, don't do that! Give me a break, Garner's the hottest thing in the damn TV world, I don't wanna be associated with trying to replace him. You can put me in his boots but I can't fill his shoes!"

But they did it, and it was okay, I didn't get damaged too much out of it, and I had some fun working on *Maverick* with Jack Kelly. He was a real pussycat, a professional, a sweet man with a great sense of humor, and no ego. I always enjoyed any time I ever spent with Jack. Our last "association" was when I went to his memorial after he died. At the time of his death he was, of all things, a city councilor or something in Huntington Beach. Here was this actor who'd had definite acclaim, but I guess it was almost a career-ending experience to have done *Maverick*, because I never heard much about him career-wise after that. Or maybe he didn't *want* to [keep concentrating on acting]. But it wasn't because he was overpaid, let me assure you *[laughs]!*

Q: Once you joined the cast of Maverick, *did your weekly paychecks improve?*

No, *nothing* changed. I was under contract to Warner Brothers. If *Maverick* had gone for a new season, of course, I would have had some bargaining chips. But by that time, the original author, the great guy Roy Huggins, was out of there. The episodes I was in weren't loaded with humor, as I recall, because we didn't have the genius of a Roy Huggins, the man who created the thing in the first place, helping us at that time. And of course Jim Garner never came back. As I told you, Jim left, and boy, with lots of chutzpah, which he always had. He ended up suing Jack Warner because I think Jack kinda put out "the word" amongst his cronies that Jim wasn't real hire-able, and that was a taboo thing to do. That's my understanding. So Jim sued Warner Brothers and the rumor I got was that he won $10 million in that lawsuit. And then he did the same thing [winning a big lawsuit] elsewhere in his career: They were messin' with on *The Rockford Files*, Jim was gettin' a bad shake on the books, and he sued and he beat them *too*. So, no, he never came back to Warners, but he walked away with more money than anybody, including Bette Davis, ever *made* out of the place *[laughs]!*

By the way, I must mention Bill Orr: He was in charge of Warner Brothers Television, he was *God* there, and I always loved him because he was fair with me. When I got the Golden Boot Award a couple of years ago [on August 10, 2002], I saw this man, almost a ghost-like figure, sitting in a wheelchair, unrecognizable. It was Bill Orr, and he was also being honored with a Golden Boot Award that night. He couldn't talk, he must have had a stroke or something, but he could listen. I went over to him with a lot of love, and I leaned down and I said, "Bill, I've always thought the world of you. You were very instrumental in helping me, putting me under contract to Warner Brothers, and so much more. I loved ya then and I love ya now." He just looked up at me

Colbert in a more recent pose.

with eyes that were totally alive — they were just dancin' around in his head with a feeling of joy, like he almost wanted to reach out and kiss me. He couldn't hardly move and he couldn't talk, but his eyes said everything. And I'm delighted to have had that moment, because a few months later he died. But I'd had that little opportunity to share my feelings with him. Bill Orr was a tough cookie, but I liked him a lot, I just thought the world of him.

Having done *Maverick* has gotten me a lot of hugs all down through my life, I get a hug from *this* person and *that* person, because I was a part of it, and there hasn't ever been one negative thing that has come of it. So how would one not associate a union like that with pleasure? *Maverick* has always been a little bouquet in my life.

Lisa Davis
THE *ENGLISH* ROSE OF TEXAS

"Give Them a Gun and the West Trembled" was one of the ad lines for The Dalton Girls. *Davis says her character in that movie "was like the female Jack Palance, really tough!"*

Born into an English show business family, Lisa Davis began her acting career as a child, then moved to America with her family at age 14 and began working in Hollywood. Two of the more offbeat roles for this English lass (then just out of her teens) were in the Westerns Fury at Gunsight Pass *(1956) and* The Dalton Girls *(1957), in which she plays the kill-crazy Rose Dalton.*

LISA DAVIS: When I was offered my first Western roles, I was already sort of familiar with Westerns, and I'd always been a big horseback rider — not that I rode in *Fury at Gunsight Pass* but I certainly did in *The Dalton Girls*. *Fury at Gunsight Pass* was with Richard Long, and we filmed at the Columbia Ranch in Burbank. Richard was a lovely, wonderful actor who had fallen in love with and married a young woman called Suzan Ball,

Lisa Davis' first Western was shot amidst the dirt — and manure — of the Columbia Ranch.

a contract player at Universal. She had done a Universal movie [*East of Sumatra*, 1953] where she was playing an island princess and she was dancing and she fell and injured her knee. The injury did not get better, and she developed cancer in that leg. So during the time she was dating Richard Long, who stood by her very faithfully, she had to have the leg amputated, which was a terrible, terrible thing. She was very young, maybe 22, and her goal was to be able to walk down the aisle on an artificial limb — which she managed to do. Of course, the whole chapel was just knocked out by it. She never got well, however, the cancer progressed, and during the time we were doing *Fury at Gunsight Pass*, she was dreadfully, dreadfully ill. I do believe she was in City of Hope, the big cancer center in Duarte, so of course Richard could never wait to get through [with each day's shooting] so that he might run to the hospital to see her. He was very, very brave, but we were all very aware of this ongoing thing, and

61

it was a sort-of tense set because of that. One night she was extremely ill, and Richard was in a terrible state the next day. And that was the day that another actor, Marshall Thompson, who was related to Richard in some way, came to the set to tell Richard that she had passed away.

One of our sets there at the Columbia Ranch was a Western-style mortuary, with coffins, and on the day that she died, I held him while he was sobbing, crying, standing there on that set, surrounded by all those wooden coffins — it was very grim. Well, he and I formed a very strong bond as friends — absolutely as *friends* — and for weeks and weeks after that picture, he would show up at my house. I lived on Franklin Avenue in Hollywood, I was then still living with my mother and father, and he would arrive in his Cadillac and he would park — I wouldn't know that he was coming — and he'd knock at the door at like ten o'clock at night and say, "Can I come in?" And with my mother, who was very, very kind, I'd sit and I'd listen to him while he would cry. Incidentally, he and his next wife Mara Corday had *legendary* fights. *Those* two, they fought and fought and fought, and she'd throw all his stuff out on the front lawn and turn on the sprinklers. They had a really tempestuous relationship! But I don't think he ever got over the Suzan Ball thing, it was such a tragedy.

Also on *Fury*, a great deal of the movie takes place during a ferocious sandstorm, so they had the wind machines on all of the time. I could never understand why they got me ready in the morning, with beautiful makeup and hair and my dress, and then we'd get out onto that set and they'd turn on the wind machines *[laughs]*, and right away I was just filthy dirty because it was kicking up all the manure from years being a ranch. We were *black* — we had it in our eyes and up our noses, and I would come home looking like I'd been in the coal mines! It was very, very unpleasant, *totally* unpleasant. One actor on it was very tough and difficult…he wasn't mean to me but he had a reputation of being very mean, and that was Neville Brand. He was a drinker, as I recall, and I think people were scared of Neville Brand much in the way people were scared of Jack Palance. For instance, if he was doing a fight, you wouldn't want to be in even a *staged* fight with Neville Brand, because he was rough. He was very kind and sweet to me, and I had a nice relationship with him, no problems, but I know that he was very tough. David Brian, the star, was very difficult and very pompous and very hard, and everything had to be just-so. His character name was Whitey, and [because he was so difficult] they would purposely misprint his name on the call sheet: Instead of Whitey, they'd put his character name down as Shitty *[laughs]*! It's true! So that's my memory of *Fury at Gunsight Pass*, that it was tough because of the death of Richard's wife and because of the wind machines and so on. But I was happy to be working, I was *thrilled* that I was working. When I see today's business, it's so different than it was then. I mean, [in the old days] we all seemed to *work* more; so few people work today. I mean, you have the top-level people working, but I know so many out-of-work actors. There seemed to be more *opportunities* to work then, I think because we made

Davis loved the location trip to Kanab, Utah, and (almost) everything else about The Dalton Girls.

more low-level, B-movies — I certainly made my share of them. There was more work, and I was consistently working, and happy to be doing *any*thing. And [on *Fury*] all the dirt washed off every night! I'd come home and get clean…and *dread* the next day *[laughs]!*

I was very, very excited about *The Dalton Girls*, I *loved* The Dalton Girls, I really did. We went on location to Kanab, Utah, for that one. Aubrey Schenck and Howard Koch, the producers, were just adorable, very, very nice to me. How they came to cast me as the heavy, I have *no* idea. In *The Dalton Girls*, I was like the female Jack Palance, really tough! And they had Les Baxter write a song which I sang in the movie, "A Gun Is My True Love."

It was a joy to go to Kanab because it was lovely. They put us up in a wonderful motel-hotel that housed all the people on the movie. But you couldn't have any alcohol there because it's Mormon, very *strict* Mormon. It was such a big deal to get a bottle of wine so you could have a glass of wine with dinner. I'm Catholic; I'm not that religious now, but during the time I was there in Kanab I was; and I remember the local Catholic priest had no church, because Kanab was such a heavily Mormon area. So this priest would deliver communion to you out of the back of his

Davis, Penny Edwards, Sue George (lying down) and Merry Anders as the Daltons, daughters of the notorious Dalton brothers.

station wagon! I liked the other "Dalton girls" very much: Merry Anders was lovely, and Penny Edwards was very, very sweet. Poor Penny, I hit her very hard in that movie. There's a scene where I was supposed to smack her around the face and I did smack her; the director Reginald LeBorg asked me to really whack her, and I did, I didn't pull it. And she was so upset! I remember that so well! Of course, in both *Dalton Girls* and *Fury at Gunsight Pass* I had to try to sound American. One of my great challenges, all of the time, was losing my [English] accent for so many different shows that I did. For one show I'd have to drop it, for the next I'd have to *use* it, for the next I'd have to do *another* accent, on and on, until I became quite fluent at changing the way I spoke; I became very good at it, actually.

The *Dalton Girls* location was a tough one because we were right out there in the dirt and the dust, with red ants climbing up our dresses. I remember being stung very badly on the legs. John Russell [the male lead] was a nice man, but the director Reginald LeBorg was a bit of a tough character. He spoke *dreadful* English, so [trying to understand] what he wanted was very difficult. For instance, if some riders came down a hill,

"No interplanetary justice, no peace!": Davis in her best-remembered movie role as one of the planet Venus' mini-skirted "freedom fighters" in Queen of Outer Space *(1958).*

he would say something like, "Those riders came down off the hill too slow too fast" *[laughs]* — which meant they came too late, and then they came too fast. I mean, you could never figure out what he was talking about! He was *so* nervous! Poor Aubrey Schenck was also always nervous; Howard Koch was much more calm.

I did a lot of my own riding in *The Dalton Girls*, and my own shooting. For the scene at the end when I'm shot and killed [in a main street shootout], they attached a very strong wire to the back of my belt, and ran it through the wall of the building a few feet behind me. When I was "shot," a grip behind the wall *yanked* on the wire, and slammed me right up against that wall. It was really quite something; it *hurt* me, actually, because it was such a wrench backwards.

Koch-Schenck *always* had a movie going; in fact, in those days, you could even shoot on a Saturday on location, and Koch-Schenck was so busy that they'd finish a movie on Saturday morning and start another one on Saturday afternoon. On the last day of *Dalton Girls*, a Saturday afternoon, most of us were sitting on a bus waiting to leave, but there were one or two more shots to go, and a second crew was waiting to start the next [Koch-Schenck] picture there. And all of a sudden, we were in the middle of a million pregnant sheep that were being moved from one place to another! Poor Aubrey Schenck was sweating bullets as we were all hopelessly delayed, waiting for these sheep to go past us!

I still *love* performing, I'm *crazy* about it, I always have been. And it was always easy for me, I was never shy, I never struggled with having to "overcome myself." I think I was an exhibitionist *[laughs]*! I really am deeply grateful that [acting] was the thing that my family chose for me to do. I love that it's given me this longevity and it's made me "different." I *like* being "different" *[laughs]*!

Maury Dexter

SAD HORSES
AND YOUNG GUNS

Maury Dexter was still a kid when his movie-loving mother decided that he wanted to be an actor and began sending him to drama classes. He went from acting to directing.

Arkansas-born Maury Dexter acted on stage, in movies and on early TV before starting to take behind-the-camera jobs in the 1950s. For Robert L. Lippert's indie outfit Regal Films (later Associated Producers) he worked in various capacities and, in the 1960s, began producing and directing many of the company's movies, including several Westerns. Here he describes making Young Guns of Texas, *an oater with the novelty of a cast largely comprised of the green-behind-the-ears offspring of established Hollywood stars.*

MAURY DEXTER: I'll tell you how the movie came about, although I'm sure anyone familiar with the way Robert Lippert worked could figure it out for themselves. Well, now, what's the title? *Young Guns of Texas.* That's a pretty good title! That was Bob Lippert's title; Lippert would come up with *all* the titles. See, Lippert was an old-time exhibitor and he knew that it didn't matter whether the title fit the subject so much, but if it was an *intriguing* title, it would bring people into the theaters. So he would think up what *he* called "intriguing titles" and give 'em to [screenwriter] Harry Spalding and say, "Write a script around it."

Anyway, Lippert came up with *Young Guns of Texas* and it was his idea to use as many "star offspring" as we could possibly get. Lippert remembered using David Ladd, the son of Alan Ladd, in a couple of pictures, *The Sad Horse* [1959] and *A Dog of Flanders* [1960], and I think that sort of influenced him to come up with other offspring of Hollywood's so-called stars in *Young Guns of Texas*. David Ladd at that particular time wasn't old enough [to play one of the Young Guns] but we got Jim Mitchum [son of Robert] and Jody McCrea [son of Joel] and David Ladd's sister Alana Ladd. She was sweet, nice and *very* pretty — she was a good combination of Alan and her mother [actress-turned-agent] Sue Carol. I loved Sue, she was a dear, dear lady, but she was *pushing* her children into acting; she was the one we went through to get Alana. If Alan had had his way, I don't think he would have wanted those kids in the business. Sue being an ex-agent and so forth, I guess she figured, "Why *not* get 'em in there?" whereas Alan was not a movie father at *all*. But Alana wasn't the greatest actress in the world and she never pursued it after that.

Q: How did you end up with Gary Conway as the third male lead instead of yet another son-of-a-star?

There *weren't* any more! And these Lippert pictures were quick pictures so we couldn't sit around and wait for somebody to be born *[laughs]!* We got who we could get! We also had Chilly Wills' boy Will, but his character was kinda "in the background," with just a couple of lines here and there. He was just "token," because Chilly (who was also in the picture) came to me one day and said, "Hey, Cuzz, *I* got a boy, too, and he's a good actor!" So I put Will in, to please Chilly, and also to help bolster the casting a little bit. It was the only movie Will was ever in; he wasn't an actor. I hadn't heard of him before, and I haven't heard of him afterwards. But he fit in, another so-called "actor's offspring."

We shot at Old Tucson Studios, on the outskirts of Tucson. It had one nice, big, workable soundstage and it had great Western streets. You could shoot in all directions because it was built out in the middle of the desert, so you didn't have to worry about trying to block [20th century] buildings. It had a wonderful main drag, and then off to the right was a whole Mexican village with all the little adobe homes and a big, beautiful, white church, and up around another corner there was another Western street that had an entirely different look — the buildings looked a *little* more modern. It was the best Western town *anywhere*, including back lots. I had already shot a few pictures there, *Walk Tall* [1960] and *The Purple Hills* [1961].

Q: The Variety *reviewer said that the youngsters in* Young Guns *"needed a firm directorial hand" and that you "didn't supply that firmness."*

Let me tell you how firm the hand was. We had Jim Mitchum, who hadn't done much yet, and Jody McCrea the same, and Alana Ladd, who had probably never been on a soundstage more than a half a dozen times during her *life*. When you have kids like these as your stars, I don't care *how* firm your hand is as a director; they either *have* it or they *don't* have it. You can work with them, which I had to do, literally work with them, in order to get what I got out of 'em. In my opinion, if they'd had a director with a firmer hand, that director wouldn't have gotten anything except, probably, sarcasm. Because these kids give you what they've *got*. You can work with people who are talented whether you're a good director or not; if they're talented, they don't *need* directors *[laughs]*. Talented actors don't need to be told what to do and how to say it and so on and so forth; they just hit their marks and they give you a performance. But not one of these kids *had* that kind of experience. What I got from them [acting-wise], except for maybe a moment or two here and there, I was perfectly happy with. I was happy to get what I *got* out of what I had to work with *[laughs]!*

Q: Did you ever meet any of these kids' fathers — Alan Ladd, Joel McCrea or Robert Mitchum?

One out of three, Alan Ladd. *The Sad Horse* with David Ladd was shot in Newhall, California, at the Disney Ranch, which had just opened, and we all stayed a few miles away at the Circle J Ranch, an exquisite dude ranch. Every night I would work with the boy for about an hour, going over the next day's lines and rehearsing him, because he had not-that-much experience — he was 11 years old. But after about the fourth or

Dexter on the set of The Sad Horse *with David Ladd, son of Alan Ladd. David went on to become a Hollywood executive.*

fifth day, the poor little guy was so homesick that it interfered with his memory. He'd go on the set and he'd freeze. The director was Jimmy Clark, who had no patience with *any*body, and he would kinda flare at the boy, and I'd say, "Jimmy, just a minute, let me talk to him…" I said to David, "Listen, David, you're gonna hafta shape up, pal, because if you don't, I'm gonna have to call your house and I don't want to do that." It was the last thing in the *world* I wanted to do, I loved this little guy, he was a sweet, honest, warm kid. Anyway, things didn't get any better, so I called and they weren't home, so I left a message with the maid or whomever, and I said, "I would suggest they come up and spend the night with David, because there's some very minor problems and I think they can help." Boy, the next day, like ten o'clock in the morning, who drove up but Alan and Sue. I said, "There's no problem, everything's fine, but…he's homesick, he misses you." Alan asked, "Maury, can you have dinner with us tonight?" So that evening David and the parents and I all went to dinner in the beautiful Circle J Ranch restaurant; and after the boy was fed and sent off to bed, Alan turned to me at the dinner table and asked, "Maury, what's the problem here?" I told Alan and Sue, "It's just that you got a boy who doesn't want to do what he's doing, he doesn't *love* it like you and *most* of us do. I try to be company to him every night but he's young and he misses *you* and he wants to be home!" So the next day, before they left, Alan called me over as he was talking to David, and Alan said, "Now, listen, son, you listen to what Maury tells you and you stay close to Maury," and blah blah blah, "and if you *don't*, I'm gonna come up here, boy, and I'm gonna…" — I don't remember, "tan your hide" or words to that effect. David started to cry, so Alan hugged him and said, "Naw, I'm not gonna do anything to you. But, for your mom's sake and my sake, come on, *do* your job now, *promise* me that." David said, "I will" — and the boy got better, he learned his lines and he hit his marks. But that's why I said before that Alan, when it came to his kids, was not a pushy guy; I don't think he relished getting the kids involved [in show biz].

The other "Young Gun," Gary Conway was a handsome type of young leading man in those days, and he did a pretty good job in the picture. He was occasionally "over," I had to bring him down a little bit — rarely, but occasionally. But in the overall, I thought he did a fairly nice job. Also in the picture, playing the heavy, was Bob Lowery, one of my favorite actors. I didn't work with him that often but I'd seen him in movies for years and I always thought he was one of the best-looking guys I'd ever seen, and equally as talented. Of course, when I used him, he was "getting up there," he was no longer the young, handsome leading man.

One day Chilly Wills came to me and he said, "Hey, Cuzz, listen, have you cast the part of the sheriff yet?" The sheriff only had three or four lines, and I was intending to pick up a local guy to do that. Chilly said, "I've got this old buddy of mine, Cuzz, and, listen, I owe him a favor," and blah blah blah, "and he's a *gooood actor*. He's as good as I am!" and so forth and so on. "And he just happens to *be* here. Let him do the sheriff! That'd

Young Guns of Texas *was stocked with the sons (and a daughter) of famous stars, giving it casting novelty. Left-right: Dexter, unidentified woman and* Young Guns *co-star Jody McCrea, son of Western great Joel McCrea.*

make that ol' boy so happy! I guarantee you, he'll do it good!" I said, "Okay, fine, Chilly, fine." A couple days later, I was shooting on the Old Tucson street, and the last shot of the last scene of the day was Bob Lowery and his henchmen riding into town. The sun had gone down and I was losing the light, and it was my last shot of the day and I knew I damn well better get it because I *needed* it, badly. I was high on a boom shooting the entire street, and we shot Lowery riding in with the henchmen trailing him on horseback, and the boom lowered down and down and I was following 'em as they rode over to the side and got off their horses, and I held the group wide and I was moving in slowly as they walked up onto the porch outside the sheriff's office. And now the sheriff, played by Chilly's old buddy "the gooood actor" [Robert Hinkle], came out onto the porch and walked up to Lowery and he was supposed to say, "Howdy, Jess. I hear you been looking for me." And instead he said, "Howdy, sheriff, I hear you been looking...[*pause*] Oh, shit, *I'm* the sheriff, ain't I?" I said, "*Cut*! Cut his *throat*!" Oh, I coulda killed him! *And* I coulda killed Chilly Wills! I almost fell off the boom! Anyway, to make a long story longer, I had to redo it instantly and I just literally got in under the wire and got the shot.

Alana Ladd, actress-daughter of Alan Ladd, behind the scenes on Young Guns of Texas *with Dexter.*

Toward the end, the Young Guns, Chilly and the girls [Ladd and Barbara Mansell as Calamity Jane] are attacked by Indians. It was 120 degrees at least in Tucson and we were in a dry sand bed, which made it even worse. Among the Indians we had little Jerry Summers and two or three of my other standby stunt guys and *they* did the stunt work, but the other Indian riders were just local [Arizona] Indians. Jody McCrea's character is killed in that scene, and then at the very end of the movie we had a scene at his graveside with Chilly [playing McCrea's father] reading the last rites, giving his son a little going-away prayer. It was a good scene; Harry Spalding wrote a really nice, warm, *sad* scene. And ol' Chilly, boy, I gotta tell you, he *delivered* it. I got the master on it, shooting Chilly and the group and the grave in the foreground, and then I started doing coverage, and the last coverage I did was on Chilly. I got a nice, big closeup of him and again he did this prayer from beginning to end. When it was over, I said *cut*, and he walked over to me and he said, "Hey, Cuzz, did you like that scene?" I said, "That was a *good scene*, Chilly. A *real* good one." He said, "Well, listen, I kinda liked that myself. You know what you could do? When you get back to the studio, what do you think about this: While this ol' boy is sayin' them good words over his poor dead son, can't you just kinda see, all of a sudden, out of nowhere, a little *halo* forms above his head…?" It took every ounce of my willpower to keep from bursting out in laughter — it was incredible! I didn't want to hurt this poor man's feelings, so I said, "Let me sleep on it, Chilly!" *[laughs]* I loved Chilly, he was one of the nicest people in the world, but…can you *imagine* coming up with an idea like that?

When I finished principal photography in Tucson, I took four or five doubles, wardrobed them, took an independent cameraman and drove back to Big Bend, Texas, and for three days I shot with these doubles on horses, in different types of terrain. I intercut all that with the rest of the picture that we'd shot in Arizona, and you never would know the difference. So the picture was shot in Arizona, principal photography, and second unit was in Big Bend, Texas.

Like every movie I've ever done, there are mistakes. Nothing major, but a few little minor things. I thought, as a production, it was a good show. We had good locations and it amply covered and I thought story-wise it worked. Twenty-some-odd years later, Fox made a movie called *Young Guns period*, again with some of the young Hollywood boys [Martin Sheen's sons Emilio Estevez and Charlie Sheen, Donald Sutherland's son Kiefer Sutherland, John Wayne's son Patrick Wayne, Jack Palance's son Cody Palance]. And *that* was a hit so Bob Lippert was right, it *is* a pretty good title!

Ed Faulkner
(AND FAMILY)
ARE *UNDEFEATED*!

Members of the cast and crew of The Undefeated *(1969): Top row, Harry Carey, Jr., Pedro Armendariz, Jr., Robert Donner, Ben Johnson, Merlin Olsen, Don Collier, Ed Faulkner; middle row, Big John Hamilton, Marian McCargo, John Wayne, Rock Hudson, Bruce Cabot, Lee Meriwether, Antonio Aguilar; bottom row, Roman Gabriel, Melissa Newman, director Andrew V. McLaglen, producer Robert L. Jacks and Jan–Michael Vincent.*

A native of Lexington, Kentucky, Ed Faulkner began his movie-TV career in the late 1950s, actively pursuing acting work for almost 18 years before moving into the business world. Six standout titles on his résumé are the movies he made for John Wayne's Batjac Productions — and for Faulkner, one of the most memorable of these was the post-Civil War actioner The Undefeated, *with Wayne as an ex-Union colonel heading a horse drive to Mexico, Rock Hudson as a Confederate colonel leading his men and their families to a new south-of-the-border future, and the dangers the two factions must face together.*

ED FAULKNER: All of Duke's films were memorable in many, many different ways. I don't think they *have* production companies like his any more; it was just a joy to be there. There was a group of us that was more or less the stock company, and I was privileged to be one of them. *McLintock!* [1963] was the first movie I did with Duke, then I did three back to back, *The Green Berets* [1968], *Hellfighters* [1968] and *The Undefeated.*

At that time [the late 1960s], I'd been away from home a *lot*, doing *Green Berets* and *Hellfighters*; back then, when making a movie, you were gone three, three and a half months at a whack. I went to Durango, Mexico, to do *The Undefeated* — and after I'd been down there a while, my family came down to Mexico too! My wife Barbara and I had three daughters and a son: Jan, who was then around 13, Barbara, who was 10, and Leslie, who was about eight. And then little Edward, or "The Caboose" as we called him. He was about a year and a half old. I'd been in Durango on *The Undefeated* about a month when Barbara called and told me she was coming down to Mexico to see me. I asked, "What about the kids?" and she said, "I'm bringin' 'em with me." I said, "*What??*" *[laughs]* She drove down, and that was an episode unto itself: We had a new Pontiac station wagon, maybe a few months old, which broke down because the differential burned out. It was quite an adventure that she went through, but they came down.

Duke knew Barbara of course, but he hadn't met our daughters. The day they first came out on the set, Duke said, "Well, get 'em in wardrobe!" It was a period piece, obviously, post-Civil War, so all the ladies were wardrobed and they started being put in the film — they actually played my family. It was a real experience for our daughters! Merlin Olsen, a dear friend of mine, a wonderful fella, *he* was down there on the movie and he did a lot of tending of my kids, and [director] Andy McLaglen's kids were there and *they* were all in the movie, and some of Duke's kids were there. They put me in a house with a coupla maids and everything, so it was really a lovely location for us.

I had such a marvelous relationship with John Wayne. He treated me almost like part of the family, almost like a son in some ways. But he never got mad at me. I remember an incident that happened on *The Green Berets*, if I can make an aside. Duke directed that of course, and there was a big closeup on me in a scene toward the end of the movie, in the tower. We did the scene a couple of times, and Duke said, "Print it." I don't know what in the world got into me — after I said this, I thought, "Oh, Jiminy Christmas!" — but I said, "Duke, can we do another one?" He looked at me and he said, "Why?" I said, "I think I'd be a little more comfortable," or what*ever* I said, I forget what it was, and he said, "Okay, let's do it again." We shot it again and he said, "Print 'em both." Now, I was never in the star category in movies, I was a character actor, sub-supporting and all that good stuff. A big star can say, "Duke, can we do one more?" but *I* had no business asking that. Anyway, I said it, I did it and it was over with. Every day they would ship the film back to Hollywood for processing and then it was sent *back* to Columbus, Georgia, Fort Benning, for Duke to look at. Duke came up to me one day after seeing rushes and he said, "You remember that scene in the tower?" He grinned and he said, "You were *right*." I don't know for sure that the extra take I asked for was the one he used in the movie — I'm gonna assume that it was — but that's the kind of a man he was.

Duke was the first man on the set and of course he knew *every single* facet and detail of moviemaking. From wardrobe to makeup to *whatever* it was, he knew it. The funny thing was, he was well-prepared, he always knew his lines, but to the best of my recollection I never saw him pick up a script. He *must* have looked at the script sometimes but I never saw him physically do that, which was kind of unusual and, I think, was interesting.

Q: Did he do any directing of the movies that he didn't "officially" direct?

In some ways. On *McLintock!* he was pretty well involved. That was Andy McLaglen's first directorial stint with Wayne as the star, and of course Andy was an integral part of the Wayne family and the company, Andy's dad Victor McLaglen having worked as many films as he did with Duke. As I recall, Wayne and Andy would work pretty closely together; I do remember, on *McLintock!*, Duke coming up to me and giving me some instructions about how to turn in a particular scene. He always had *some*thing to say. And if he didn't like something, I'm sure he would take the director aside.

The weather was super in Durango on *The Undefeated*. That's great country down there. It's open country, no telephone poles, the skies are usually pretty clear. But we were down there in late January-February-March 1969, something like that, so we would have some cool mornings. I had a polo coat, which is a double-breasted camelhair coat, belted across the back. I wore it for warmth because, as I say, mornings *would* be cold.

Faulkner as Capt. Anderson in The Undefeated, *one of six John Wayne movies in which he appears. The actor says that Wayne "treated me almost like part of the family, almost like a son in some ways."*

I had this coat on one morning, heavy, good and warm. Occasionally when we were on location, the Stetson hat people would arrange to come out and bring I-don't-know-*how*-many-different hats, and Duke would model them in photographs. This one morning, Duke came up to me and he said, "Can I ask you a favor? That coat you're wearing is the best-looking coat they ever made. If you'd let me borrow it, I could wear it in some of these pictures…" So I took off the coat, and held it up for him to put on. He stuck one arm in it, and he got the other arm in the other sleeve, and I could see and actually *hear* the seams popping *[laughs]!* He couldn't get into it, he was so big. Boy he was big, Jiminy Christmas…! He had the biggest, deepest chest of any man I've ever seen. And he kept himself in pretty good shape thanks to Ralph Volkie. Ralph was part of Duke's company and would travel with Duke. He was a masseur, and occasionally would have a small part in a picture. Incidentally, in terms of height, I was the smallest principal on that movie, and I'm 6'3"! Duke was 6'4", Rock was 6'4", Merlin was 6'5", Roman Gabriel was 6'3" or 6'4" — and Andy McLaglen was six foot *seven [laughs]!* They were just big people!

The stampede scenes in *The Undefeated* were interesting because I'd never seen horses that small. I don't know if they were exclusive to Mexico, but they were some kind of a breed that's not a full-sized horse. Fifteen, sixteen hands is a good-sized horse; I think one of the Derby horses was 17 hands, and that's a *big* horse. These *Undefeated* horses must have been 12, 13 hands — diminutive! But the thing is, when you watch a film, unless those horses are standing up next to a "regular-size" horse, or next to something you *know* the size of, like a particular car, you have no idea of their size. I watched a lot of those stampede scenes being shot, and that was thrilling.

The Wayne stock company regulars were a good group of people. In *The Undefeated* they had ol' Ben Johnson, what a love *he* was; "Dobe" Carey; Gregg Palmer, another good friend of mine; Bruce Cabot…Bruce played my father in *McLintock!*, and he was also in *Berets*, *Hellfighters*, *Undefeated* and *Chisum*. Duke kind of "took care" of Bruce.

Q: Did Bruce Cabot need taking care of?

I mean financially, because Bruce didn't do a lot of work in his latter days. I loved Bruce, he and I got along fine. Duke called him "The Indian" because he was part-Cherokee or something. The funny thing about Bruce was that, with him, it was either *black* or *white*, there apparently was no in-between. Let's say he liked me, and let's say that Bruce and I were having a conversation and "Joe Blitzflitz" walked up — and Bruce doesn't like "Joe Blitzflitz." Well, Bruce would turn around in mid-sentence and just walk away. Unless you *knew* him well, some people didn't know how to "take" him. And, yes, he drank. I remember we were up in Casper, Wyoming, doing *Hellfighters*. Duke loved to play bridge, he was a very good bridge player, and it was a Sunday up in Casper, where for excitement you watch the washing machine or something *[laughs]*. My hotel room was down the hall from Duke's, and late one Sunday morning there was a knock on the door and I opened it and there he was. He asked, "Do you and Barbara have any plans today?" We didn't. He said, "Listen, grab a fourth, I'll get the Indian, come on down to my suite and we'll play some bridge." Alberto Morin loved to play bridge, he was a nice guy, and so it was Alberto and Duke and Barbara and myself playing bridge — and "The Indian" stayed over in a corner playing solitaire and sipping his vodka or gin or whatever it was. Bruce was a character.

After we finished shooting in Durango, the company moved to Baton Rouge, Louisiana, and we were there, I think, a coupla weeks, filming primarily the opening scenes where Rock Hudson's mansion is burned and all of that. Again Barbara and our girls, Jan, Barbara and Leslie, were with me, and again they joined me on-screen. For appearing in the picture while we were in Mexico, the kids were paid some kind of a pittance of a wage, and they ate that up. But when we got to Baton Rouge, back in the jurisdiction of the various unions, Barbara, God bless her, went to one of the production people and said, "Now look, we're back in the States, you pay these kids some more money" — and they did! I've forgotten how much, but it was a considerable amount more than what they'd been making in Mexico. They thoroughly enjoyed that!

Q: Rock Hudson being gay — how open a secret was that at the time you made The Undefeated?

I'm sure everybody was aware, I'm sure Duke was aware, but it was never talked about. He and Duke got along fine; in fact, they sometimes used to play bridge together in the evenings while we were on location. Rock was a great big, good-looking guy, and *such* a nice person. One afternoon, it may have been a Saturday, everybody was off work and we were at the hotel in Baton Rouge lounging around the pool. Rock was lying in a deck chair in a bathing suit. Our three daughters went up to him with cameras and they said, "Mr. Hudson, would you mind if we got a photograph of you?" and he said, "Of course not." He kind of straightened up, got ready, and the girls got right up close to his face for a closeup, and their "cameras" were water guns *[laughs].* Barbara and I were in on the gag, watching from the background, and it was so funny to see! He was absolutely stunned when this happened! The girls screamed with laughter, and he got up off the deck chair and started chasin''em! It was a cute situation.

Faulkner's real family became his "reel family" in The Undefeated: *wife Barbara and daughters Jan, Barbara and Leslie.*

Rock was down to earth and really great with everybody. In fact, everybody had gotten so friendly that one day when three or four of us were sitting around talking with him in Baton Rouge, he said, "Listen, after the film, when we get back [to California], I want you all to come up to my house and have dinner. We'll screen my copy of *Giant* [1956]." A lot of times on pictures, people will say things like that and they don't follow through. But after the picture was finished and I was back home, I was out in our front yard one day mowing the grass and my daughter Barbara came out and said, "Dad, guess who's on the phone! It's Mr. Hudson!" — and he was calling to invite us over to see *Giant*! Barbara and I and Bob Donner, a dear friend of mine who was also on *The Undefeated*, and his wife at that time Cissy Wellman, and I think Merlin and Sue Olsen, and there may have been another couple, we went up to his charming two-bedroom house in Beverly Hills, and had a wonderful Mexican dinner which he had prepared for us, and then we sat there and he screened *Giant*. Before many of the scenes, he would stop the projector and he'd say, "Now, let me tell you, the night before shooting this scene was the first time I'd met Liz Taylor and we got drunk and…" etc., etc., and then he'd restart the projector. It was fun to hear those stories from Rock. He was just a nice person, he really and truly was.

An aside: Another picture I did with Duke was *Hellfighters*, and one day between scenes Duke came up to me and he said, "Listen, I just read a script and it's gonna be a helluva picture, and there's a damn good part you'd be right for. Let me see what I can do." Well, the movie was *True Grit* [1969], and the part he wanted *me* for was the part of the young sheriff. Of course, I didn't get the part; I didn't have a name and Glen Campbell was very prominent. I'm *not* trying to knock Campbell, but he was under contract to the producer Hal Wallis and so he did the part, and…well, he just wasn't an actor. Not that I could have done it any better, but he was miscast, in my estimation. (And that's not just because I would have loved to do the part!)

I was in the business in a wonderful era. Westerns were prominent, and I was big and could ride a horse, and I had some marvelous times. I was actively pursuing [an acting career] for 18, almost 19 years, and then for some personal reasons I got out of it and went into the legitimate business world. (Having *been* in films helped me a great deal there.) Over the last four or five years, I've been doing a little work occasionally. I don't have a real theatrical agent per se; my agent is the lovely wife of Jon Provost from *Lassie*, and she promotes a lot of people for festivals and so on. Earlier this year [2009] she got me a voiceover job as a Christmas elf on an animated cartoon called *Elf Sparkle Meets Christmas the Horse*! Incidentally, for the next *Elf Sparkle* episode, I am to direct the voice actors, including Margaret O'Brien as Mrs. Claus!

Barbara and I recently celebrated our 55th wedding anniversary. We were only five when we got married *[laughs]*.

Behind the scenes with (right to left) Faulkner, director Andrew V. McLaglen and Rock Hudson. Faulkner grew the beard for the movie and briefly kept it after production wrapped.

Q: You say that as a joke but since you were born on a February 29, a Leap Year, you're probably not far off!

Last year I celebrated my 19th Leap Year birthday. Back around that time, I ran into a man and we got to talking about birthdays, and I said, "Well, I was born on a leap year and this year I'm gonna be 19." He looked at me and he said, "Let me tell you something: For a 19-year-old, you look terrible!" I almost fell down laughing! When I was eight, which would have made me 32, Barbara had a birthday party for me, and there were five or six couples we invited to our house in Hollywood, and everybody came dressed *as* eight-year-olds. And Barbara and I dressed as eight-year-olds, too; I had on short pants and so on. We played eight-year-old games and I got some marvelous eight-year-old gifts, including a Flintstones car. So I've had a lot of fun with that.

Q: What's your favorite John Wayne memory?

There were *so* many moments, but I'll tell you about a situation on *The Green Berets*: Two of our first three children had already been born by cesarean section, and now our last child was to be taken by cesarean. The baby was going to be born on August 21, 1967, while I was in Columbus, Georgia, doing *Green Berets*, and of course I didn't know where I would be on that day or what the situation was going to be. And this was long before cell phone days. Barbara and I made a plan: She was going to deliver in St. John's Hospital in Santa Monica and I said, "I will attempt to call you at noon West Coast time," which was 3:00 in Georgia. At noon she was going to be in recovery and in a position where she could talk. Well, of course on that day, we were out at what we referred to as "the A Camp," about an hour and a half out of Columbus where we were housed; the A Camp was kind of a rough, scrubby area, supposed to be Vietnam in the movie. Around two-ish, after lunch, I kind of wandered off, thinking to myself, "Oh boy, this isn't gonna work…" when I felt an arm come around my shoulder. I looked, and it was Wayne, and in that wonderful voice of his he said, "You're supposed to be makin' a phone call…" I stammered out *something*, I don't remember what — I was so stunned that he even knew about this. (I'd mentioned it to Jim Hutton so I think Hutton must have told him.) And with that, he turned me around just as his driver George Coleman was bringing up Duke's car, his Pontiac station wagon with the big bubble on the top so Duke could sit in there with his hat on. Duke said, "George'll get ya back," and he put me in that car, and I think Coleman broke every traffic law in the state of Georgia and he got me back to my little apartment in Columbus in time to make that phone call and find out that my son had been born and that Barbara was okay.

So there was *that* side of Wayne: He was very much a family man, he loved his family, he was very caring, and that's a tender memory. The next day, back at the A Camp, I was passing out cigars; Duke had stopped smoking, but he was chewing tobacco so I proffered a cigar to him, saying, "Duke, I know you're not smoking any more, but you can chew on this thing." He said, "Chew, hell. Where's your lighter?" and he smoked it. He was a marvelous, wonderful person. I just loved the man. There'll never be another John Wayne. He made *so* many fine movies — *The Quiet Man* [1952], *The Searchers* [1956], on and on. Two years ago, when I was in Winterset, Iowa, his birthplace, celebrating what would have been his centennial birthday, a poll came out rating the world's most popular actors. He'd been gone 28 years and yet he was the third most popular film actor in the *world*, 28 years after his death. He just had a presence on the screen that will never be duplicated.

Andrew J. Fenady
REVISITS *THE REBEL*

Andrew J. Fenady (right) with the star of The Rebel, *Nick Adams. Fenady loosely based Adams' TV character on Jack London, an author for whom Fenady has such a fascination that he's since written and produced a 1993 TV version of London's* The Sea Wolf *and written the book* The Summer of Jack London.

A series that sits like a crown atop the mountain of vintage TV Westerns,
The Rebel *(1959-61) starred Nick Adams as an ex-Confederate soldier roam-*
ing the post-Civil War West, writing a book about the things he learns and
feels. The character-driven series was an early highlight in the long career of
writer-producer Andrew J. Fenady.

Fenady's first Hollywood credits, made in collaboration with director Irvin
Kershner, were the 60 Minutes-*like TV series* Confidential File *and the*
indie feature Stakeout on Dope Street *(1958). At his next stop, Paramount,*
Fenady had his initial encounters with Adams, soon to attain small-screen star-
dom as the panther-quick, leather-tough Johnny Yuma of Fenady-Kershner's
debut TV series...

ANDREW J. FENADY: At Paramount, Irv Kershner and I shot a low-budget picture called *The Young Captives* [1959]. It was very well-received and we brought it in under budget and they liked us at Paramount. At that point, I began working on a war picture that was going to star Harry Guardino and Fess Parker; I was working on *The Syndicate Executioner*, a feature for Dick Powell's company Four Star (Dick wanted to get Jimmy Cagney, a friend of his, to play the lead); and I got an option on the book *The Execution of Private Slovik* by William Bradford Huie. [Eddie Slovik was a real-life World War II soldier court-martialed and sentenced to death for desertion.] Niven Busch and I were going to write the screenplay. Louella Parsons wrote in her column about Fenady-Kershner making *The Execution of Private Slovik* with Paul Newman, and after her item appeared, I got a letter from Nick Adams, a guy I had seen a few times at the Beverly Hills gym where I worked out. Nick wrote, "I know you've got Paul Newman, but in case anything happens to Paul Newman, I've got to play the part of Slovik. Slovik was Polish. I'm Polish. Slovik was from Detroit. I'm from Detroit." Well, the first part was the truth, he *was* Polish, but Nick was not from Detroit, he was from New Jersey! Well, he'd *lived* in New Jersey but that isn't where he was born, he was born in Nanticoke, Pennsylvania.

Anyhow, Nick said, "Have lunch with me. I'll buy you lunch. I want to meet you. We've got to get together." He gave me his phone number so I called him up and I said, "Okay, fine, I'll meet you at Oblath's [restaurant]." So we went to Oblath's, across the street from Paramount, and he was giving me all this business about *Private Slovik*, and I said, "Nick, I got news for you. We're not gonna make *Private Slovik*." The president then was Eisenhower, he was the last guy who could have said, "No, don't shoot the son of a bitch," but he *didn't* say no so they shot Slovik and nobody in this town wanted to touch it at that time.

But Nick and I got to be pals, and he started getting after me, like at a New Year's Eve party: "Andy, Andy, do a pilot for me, do a pilot for me. I'm good, I'm a hell of an actor. Do a pilot!" I said, "What the hell do you want to *do*, Nick?" and he said, "Well, I dunno. Like a Jimmy Cagney [a vehicle for a Cagney type]." He did a lot of Jimmy Cagney and Cary Grant imitations, stuff like that. Well, he couldn't be Cary Grant but he *thought* he could be Jimmy Cagney. He said, "Cagney made a picture called *Johnny Come Lately* [1943]. Why don't we do something like that?" I said, "Nick, let me tell you something: Of the top ten shows on television, *seven* of them are Westerns. We ain't gonna do *Johnny Come Lately*." So I sat down and in three days I wrote a half-hour pilot which at that time was called *The Journal of Johnny Yuma* [later changed to *The Rebel*]. I had never written a Western before, but I had seen practically every Western that was ever made while I was a kid and I loved all the Tom Mixes and the John Waynes and the Randolph Scotts.

Nick and I took *The Rebel* to Dick Powell because, back at the time when Dick and I were going to do *The Syndicate Executioner*, Dick had said to me, "I know you want to do features, Andy, but in the meantime, if you ever have a television project, bring it to me. Will you promise to do that?" I said, "You bet, sir." So Nick and I took the *Rebel* script to him, and he read it and he said, "Holy mackerel, you know what? We're gonna do this on *Zane Grey Theater* as a pilot, next season. We're all booked up this season, but *next* season, that's what we're gonna do. We'll do *The Rebel* and I'm gonna sell it for us." Great!

Meanwhile, Irv Kershner did for [executive producers] Mark Goodson and Bill Todman the first episode of the TV series *Philip Marlowe*. While he was there, there was a fellow working for Goodson-Todman, in charge of development, called Harris Katleman. Katleman said to Kersh, "Hey, you and your partner, have you got any Westerns?" Kersh said, "Well, yeah, A.J. Fenady wrote a Western. We've got a deal for it, but if you want to call and talk to him, go ahead." So Katleman called me up and he asked about *The Rebel* and he asked if he could read it. I said, "Look, we're gonna do it with Powell, but if you want to read it, you can read it. And if you like it, I'll write *another* one for you." He said, "Great, great," so I sent it to him and he read it and he called me back up a couple of days later and he said, "How much will it take to shoot this pilot?" I didn't know how much but I grabbed a figure, I said, "$50,000." He said, "I'll get back to you." When he got back to me, he said, "Goodson and Todman will put up $50,000 today. Fifty-fifty, partners, you and them. How does that strike you?" I said, "Jesus, we can't do this. Dick Powell said he was going to do *The Rebel* next year." Katleman said, "I'm talkin' about *now*."

So Nick and I went over to see Dick Powell, and I told him what happened. Dick said, "Andy. Nick. Don't hesitate. Who knows what's gonna happen with *Zane Grey Theater* between now and then? Go ahead and shoot it. Take it and God bless you, I wish you all the luck in the world. Do it! Do it! *Do it now!*" He was a wwwwonderful man, just a great, great man. So I went back to Goodson-Todman and I said, "Okay, let's go," and we shot it. But it wasn't *quite* that easy. Here's a story that I don't think has been printed before...

After Goodson and Todman agreed to do it, Katleman called me and he said, "Andy, we've got a problem. Mark and Bill don't think that Nick is right." I said, "What do you mean he's not right? I *wrote* it for him." He said, "They just ran *No Time for Sergeants* [a 1958 comedy with Andy Griffith as a hayseed drafted into the Air Force and Adams as a "four-eyed" fellow inductee]. Christ Almighty, he's a sidekick in it, a skinny little guy, a *comic. He* can't play the Rebel!" So I called up Nick and I said, "Nick, you ever done a Western?" He said, "Yeah, yeah, yeah, I did one with John Derek. It was called *Fury at Showdown* [1957]." So I called those guys back and I said, "Nick's done Westerns. He did *Fury at Showdown* with John Derek." They said, "Can we see it?" So I got the goddamn picture and sent it to them in New York, and they were going to run it two or three mornings later and then call me. They ran it and they called me, a conference call. I said, "Mark? Bill? Harris? Did you see *Fury at Showdown* with Nick and John Derek?" They said yes. I said, "Well, what do you think?" They said, "Get *John Derek* to play the Rebel!" *[laughs]* I said, "No, fellas, we're not gonna get John Derek to play the Rebel. It's either Nick, or else we'll go back to Dick Powell." So they said *[grudgingly]*, "Well...okay...go ahead and shoot the goddamn thing." So we shot *The Rebel* and, well, that's how *The Rebel* came about. We shot the pilot in four days, the rest of the episodes were shot in three days. And Dan Blocker was in the pilot; I paid him $80 a day for three days, and the next week he did the pilot of *Bonanza* and never stopped working after that. And we never stopped being pals until the day he died.

I gave Nick "co-creator" credit on *The Rebel* because...welllll, because he was telling everybody about it, "Fenady and I are working on it," "Fenady and I are working on it," and I said to myself, "Oh, what the hell, what do I care?" He was a nice guy, a sweet guy, and I had a feeling that I was going to go on and create a helluva lot of other things and I didn't figure *he* was gonna "create" many more series *[laughs]*. I figured, "It won't do *me* any harm and it might do him some good," so I gave him the credit. Actually, it wasn't until the second season that I finally *told* Nick how I got the idea for the series. One day I said to him, "Nick, you know who we're doing?" and he said, "Yeah, we're doin' the Rebel!" I said, "No, listen, I'll tell you where I really got this idea…" The fact is, I did a lot of research and I became fascinated with the character of Jack London. I based the Rebel on Jack London, a restless young man who wanted to be a writer, but he couldn't write it unless he lived it. *That's* the advice that Jack London got from a librarian [Ina Coolbrith] and that's what he did: He became a seaman and he wrote about the sea. He became a miner in Alaska and he wrote about mining, and on and on. *All* the things that he wrote about, he learned how to do 'em while he was traveling. Like the Rebel, London didn't stay in one place; there was always another horizon, there was always another mountain to climb.

Another thing that distinguished the Rebel was the cap that he wore. In my pilot script, I wrote that he was wearing the cap when he came back to Mason City and avenged the death of his father. Then at the end of the script, I had him take off the cap and put on his father's hat [which he was going to wear from then on]. As we were rehearsing, Nick put the father's hat on and he looked at himself in the mirror and he turned around and he looked at me. I knew what he was thinking. I shook my head and I said, "Nick, put that goddamn cap back on." He took that hat off and put the cap back on and we *stuck* with the cap. A lot of things distinguished the Rebel, but that cap also. Whenever he rode into a town or walked into a room, he wasn't like the other TV cowboys, Wyatt Earp and Lawman and Cheyenne and all those guys. You could tell that he was something set apart.

Another thing Johnny Yuma wore was an eagle claw, on a cord around his neck. Western Costume is right down the block from Paramount, so Nick and I went over there and I said, "Hey, you got any eagle claws?" One guy said, "Come on, follow me," so we went upstairs and he opened up a drawer, and in there were about 15 or 20 eagle claws. Nick and I started inspecting them, picking out shapes and sizes, and I said, "We'll buy one of 'em. No, we'll buy a *couple* of 'em, so we'll have a back-up in case we lose one." He said, "Oh no you won't. You can't buy any of those eagle claws. It's an endangered species and we can't get any more. We will *rent* them to you." I said, "But we want to use it on the whole *series*," and he said, "Well…then rent it." He said the rental on each claw would cost us 25 bucks, 50 bucks a week, I forget. I mulled it over and I said, "Look, I tell you what, we'll get back to you on this, okay?" The guy went about his business, Nick and I went about our business, we walked out of Western Costume, started walking back toward Paramount...*[pause]*...and I said, "Nick..." He said, "Yeah?" I said, "How many did you get?" He said, "I got two." I said, "I got *three*!" *[laughs]* So we had our eagle claws!

Mark Goodson and Bill Todman were our financiers and partners on *The Rebel*. Bill was the businessman, and Mark considered himself the creative genius. Mark was a good guy, but he was a little fella. This'll tell you everything you need to know: He had a small statue of Napoleon on his desk *[laughs]*! Mark did everything except walk around with his hand stuck in the front of his vest! Talking about *The Rebel*, he'd say to me, "There are certain things that we have to define. Number one, *why* is he called the Rebel? Is it because he fought for the South, or is it because he had a rebellious nature?" I said, "Markie...*[pause]*...let's not overanalyze this stuff. He's the Rebel and that's it, don't look at it too closely." Now, as far as being a rebel goes, Johnny Yuma wasn't vituperative, and he didn't go around picking fights or looking for revenge. He lost a cause and he gained an insight. Actually, in the first episode ["Johnny Yuma"], when Yuma comes back to his home town after fighting in the Civil War, Jeanette Nolan [playing his aunt] says to him, "Don't tell me you went to fight for a cause. You didn't know what a cause *was*. You were just running away." That was true. So Yuma was not a bitter sort of a fellow. He wanted to learn, and his two heroes were his late father the sheriff, who stood for law and order, and Elmer Dodson [John Carradine], editor of the newspaper in his home town. Throughout the series, Yuma kept sending Elmer Dodson things that he had written, because [in "Johnny Yuma"] Dodson said about Yuma's writings, "They're crude but poetic. You've got a certain talent, but you can't write it unless you *live* it, John." So Yuma started to keep a journal and to write things and to send 'em back to Elmer Dodson.

This was the important thing about that series: When writers would come in to me to make a pitch, they'd say, "Okay, A.J., lemme tell you what it's about..." I'd say, "Wait a minute, pal. Don't tell me *what* it's about. Tell me *who* it's about." (Or, if they were educated, I'd say, "Tell me *whom* it's about!") I can make a plot out of any goddamn thing. There are only so many plots. Some people say there are nine plots. Some people say there are seven plots. Some people say there's *one* plot: Somebody loses something. Or, conversely, somebody *finds* something, as in John Steinbeck's *The Pearl*. What I wanted from these writers was, "Give me a character that I can believe in. A character I want to know more about." I would *always* look for *characters*. Then also, I would always try to put into each episode some kind of a bit of philosophical quotation, whether it was from the Bible or Shakespeare or wherever, a line that you could remember and you could learn from. That kind of writing is what differentiated *The Rebel*.

Q: One classic Rebel *episode, "Night on a Rainbow" with James Best, is about Civil War-related drug addiction.*

"There was never anybody like Nick [Adams]. Never anybody more cooperative," Rebel *creator-producer Fenady (right) says of the actor playing the starring role of Johnny Yuma.*

When guys would shoot up with dope [in the 1950s], that's what they said they were doing, spending "a night on a rainbow." I thought "Night on a Rainbow" would be a helluva title. So I used it on an episode of the TV series *Confidential File*, and when I was doing the movie [that became] *Stakeout on Dope Street,* I wanted to use it again. But Roger Corman [part-financier of *Stakeout*] and also some other guys said to me, and rightly so, "A.J.! *Night on a Rainbow*? It sounds like a goddamn MGM musical!" *[laughs]* For the writing of the *Rebel* episode "Night on a Rainbow," the [on-screen] credit goes to Peggy and Lou Shaw, but they handed in a script and…at that time they didn't know much about dope and things like that. So I sat down and did a *lot* of work on that script. As a matter of fact, it won some kind of an award, a Western Spur award or some goddamn thing. Afterwards, Peggy and Lou came to me and said, "Andy, we want to thank you for shooting this exactly the way we wrote it!" *[laughs]* Jesus!

While we were doing *The Rebel*, I was on the set *all* the time. We shot these things in three days, $40,000 per episode. We would shoot one day on a nearby location, which would be upper Iverson's or lower Iverson's or Thousand Oaks or wherever the hell it was; then we'd shoot one day on the Western street at Paramount; and then we'd shoot one day of interiors on the lot, and it would be a jail or a bar or a ranch house or whatever the hell. When we would shoot the first day out on location, we would get on a bus or in a stretch-out and it'd take about an hour to get there from Paramount. Well, Nick had bought a house in the suburbs, and instead of coming down to Paramount, he would have us pick him up. Our car would get off the freeway and head down there, and by then Nick had parked his car at a gas station on the corner and he'd be standing there with his makeup already on, in his Rebel outfit! He'd have everything but his gun, because he couldn't take his gun home. We'd slow down, he'd jump in the damn car and, zoom, off we would go. We'd get the day's work and then, on the way back to Paramount, we'd dump him off again at the same place!

Sometimes, when we were a little bit behind schedule, I would *not* shoot Nick's close-ups. Then after we did five or six episodes with*out* many of his closeups, and we had a little time, I'd say, "Okay, Nick, now we're gonna make up for that stuff that we didn't shoot." I would sit off-camera and read him his cues. He'd say, "Who am I talkin' to now?" I'd say, "You're talkin' to Agnes Moorehead." "Okay. What's the line?" So I'd give him the line and he'd proceed to play the scene with me as Agnes Moorehead. Next he'd play another scene with me as Claude Akins. He'd play each scene with me as whoever the hell it was. That's the kind of a guy he was, he didn't give a damn. There was never anybody like Nick. Never anybody more cooperative. Another thing: Nick was not a big fella, he was 5'8" tall. When we'd be casting, and I'd think about using somebody like, say, Charles Maxwell who was tall, it would occur to me that Nick was 5'8" but Nick would say, "What do *I* care?" Or I'd want to use Claude Akins, another big guy, and Nick's attitude was still, "What do *I* care? I'm the Rebel! I can lick *any*body!" The bigger they were, the better he liked it!

We had a great makeup man named Beau Hickman, and Nick would say, "Beau, Beau! Put a little D.C. on me." You know what D.C. stood for? "Dark Chin"! He had a great jaw, prominent bone structure, but he wanted to accentuate it even *more* by darkening his throat so the chin would be even more prominent! There was nobody like him, he was great.

Nick did a lot of his own stunt stuff, but we also had different guys stunt-doubling him. I think, a couple of times, Bob Miles doubled him, and even Hal Needham; we used Hal an awful lot. Richard Farnsworth doubled him a few times, too. Farnsworth was a good guy and a helluva stuntman, and he became a helluva actor. In an episode that I wrote called "Yellow Hair," Nick is alone in the desert and he comes across this fellow on a horse, a soldier wearing just the remnants of a uniform, and he's injured and all sunburned. Nick walks up to him and touches him, and the soldier falls off the horse and, before he dies, he says, "Fort Concho." That soldier was Dick Farnsworth. Well, when we shot that scene, as Farnsworth fell off the horse, he kicked Nick in the head, and goddamn nearly knocked him out *[laughs]*. Afterwards, every time I'd see Farnsworth, he would say "Fort Concho!" and he'd kick his foot to remind me of how he kicked Nick in the head!

In those days, all the Western shows would have theme songs, *Lawman*, *Cheyenne*, all those guys. So I said, "Okay, I'm gonna write a *Rebel* theme song." To write the music I used Dick Markowitz, who had already done *Stakeout on Dope Street* and *The Young Captives* for me, and I wrote the lyrics. Now we had to find somebody to sing it. You know who was hot at the time, was the Ames Brothers, so Markie Goodson and Bill Todman kept saying to me, "We can get the Ames Brothers." I said, "I don't want the Ames Brothers. First of all, *one* guy should sing this. The show's about a guy called the Rebel, *one man*. I don't want three brothers to do the damn thing." At the time, not too many people knew who the hell Johnny Cash was but I did, and I took one of his records home to my wife Mary Frances and I said, "Listen to this guy…" She knows music pretty good, and she said, "Oh, Andy, my *God*, he's flat. Oh, he's *so* flat. He can't hit a note!" I said, "I don't care, baby, if he's flat or square or circle or triangular or whatever the hell he is. *I love that voice.*" I called Johnny up — he lived out here in the Valley — and we got together, and I said, "Johnny, we'd love for you to do this." He said, "Sure, sure, I'll do it!" — he was glad to get the work. Then he said, "Mr. Fenady...could I also have a part?" I said, "You betcha!"

Adams, making a public appearance at the Corriganville Movie Ranch, is introduced by the tourist attraction's owner, actor Ray "Crash" Corrigan.

But as wonderful as he was, the son of a gun couldn't get the lyrics straight. I'd say to him, "Look, I don't care if you say 'Johnny Yuma was a rebel, he roamed through the west' or 'Johnny Yuma *is* a rebel, he *roams* through the west.' But you *can't* say, 'Johnny Yuma *was* a rebel, he *roams* through the west!' You can't mix up the tenses!" He'd try it again and I'll be damned if he didn't do it wrong again! So when the show first went on the air, it went on with the song *wrong* [with the tenses mixed up] for a while! But then later we re-recorded it, I think when Johnny came in to do a part as I'd promised him [in the episode "The Death of Gray"], and he finally got it right. That song is included in his various albums and I made a *fortune* from royalties. I met him again years later, when we were giving him a Golden Boot, and I said, "I want you to know that you put all six of my kids through college with that song." He said, "I hope I put your *grand*children through, too, Mr. Fenady!" He was terrific!

Elvis Presley visited the *Rebel* set quite often — not every *day*, but while he was shooting on the lot, he would stop by to see Nick Adams, and then I got to know him too. He would call you sir — "yes sir," "no sir." A very courteous gentleman, very, very sweet. And at that time I had an idea which is *still* a great idea: Do *Beau Geste* as a Western with Elvis Presley playing the Gary Cooper part and Nick Adams playing another brother and somebody else, Mark Goddard or somebody, playing the third brother. Unfortunately, it never worked out, Elvis was under contract to Hal Wallis, and Col. Parker was involved, and so on and so forth. [According to an April 3, 1959, *Hollywood Reporter* item, Presley had just recorded a theme song for *The Rebel*.] That's not true. It was probably planted in the *Reporter* by my publicist David Epstein.

During that time and after that time, for quite a while, Nick and Elvis and I worked out at the Paramount gym. That gym had originally been a barn on Selma and Vine Street, and then it became the Lasky-DeMille studio where in 1914 *The Squaw Man* [Hollywood's first feature] was produced. DeMille had that barn-turned-studio moved over onto the lot and had it declared a historical site so nobody could tear it down! I'll tell you who was working out there at Paramount in the old "Squaw Man" barn: There was Elvis Presley, Nick Adams, Steve McQueen, Dan Blocker, Michael Landon and me. We were all working out there and, do you want me to tell you something? I'm the only one who's still alive. A lot of 'em died young.

I loved that Paramount lot. First of all, it was right close to my house *[laughs]*, and second of all, there was a man there named Frank Caffey who was in charge of production, a wonderful, wonderful man. When I first went to Paramount, I had never made a real feature (*Stakeout on Dope Street* was a goddamned bootlegged thing), and Frank Caffey showed me the ins and outs of making a picture affiliated with a studio. And he told me, "Andy, if you ever get anything else, bring it to Paramount and I'll give you the best." He was a graduate of West Point, he was Cecil B. DeMille's right hand for a few years, and then he took over the studio as

In the comedic Rebel *episode "The Earl of Durango," Fenady made a gag appearance as District Marshal Hondo Payne — dressed (and accompanied by a dog) like John Wayne in* Hondo, *and using Wayne's* The Searchers *catchphrase "That'll be the day."*

far as production goes. He had a son, Dick Caffey, who became my unit manager, and another son, Michael, who I made a first assistant director. I first worked with Frank on *The Young Captives* and then *The Rebel*, and I stayed there at Paramount for years and years; for instance, I had a deal where I did, between the first and second season of [Fenady's 1965-66 TV series] *Branded*, a feature with Columbia and Goodson-Todman called *Ride Beyond Vengeance* [1966] and we shot that whole thing at Paramount because of Frank Caffey.

Nick met [actress] Carol Nugent around the time of *The Rebel*, and one day he came to me and he said, "I'm gonna get married!" That was great; I'd met Carol two or three times. Then he asked, "A.J., where did you go on your honeymoon?" I said, "Mary Frances and I went up to Lake Arrowhead for two, three days." (As a matter of fact, I was then working on *Confidential File*, and while we were up there I had to write an episode called "Sexual Incompatibility in Marriage"!) Anyway, I told him Lake Arrowhead and he said, "Okay, that's where I'm gonna take Carol. I'm gonna go up to Arrowhead, just like you did. And, listen — why don't you come up there with us?" I said, "Nick! On your *honeymoon*? Are you crazy? *No*!" He said, "Aww, come on, come on!" I said, "I tell you what: You go up there for two or three days, and then if you want, gimme a call and we'll come up and spend a day or two with you." And that's what we did!

Q: Why did such a great show only last two seasons?

The Rebel was the most popular show ABC had on Sunday night. As a matter of fact, I think it was the only show that wasn't done by Warner Brothers — all the other ones, the *Mavericks* and *Lawmans* and *Colt .45s* that were on Sunday, were all Warner Brothers. So ABC and Goodson-Todman came to me and said, "Do another Western. We'll get it on," and I said all right. So I came up with another one, and I told 'em, "I've got another Western for you and — you won't believe this — it's called *The Yank*." I thought it was one of the best ideas that I ever had for television: It was about a young doctor who, when his father is killed at Fredericksburg, says, "The hell with this." He puts down the scalpel, picks up a sword, joins Sherman and cuts a swath of death through the South. When the war's over, he realizes that he's got to make amends some way, so he's going to trace his route through the South and, instead of killing Southerners, he's going to help them in any way he can. I got Jimmy Drury — I'd used him in a couple of *Rebel* episodes — and I dressed him up the way that I would dress him as the Yank. We shot a pilot, and it turned out just great.

Bill Todman made a deal with ABC that if they picked up the *Yank* pilot, they had to give us [a commitment for] 39 episodes. But when ABC saw it, they said, "This is *good*. It's *so* good, here's what we're gonna do: Not only do we want to put this on the air, but we don't want to put it on next year, we want to put it on *this* year. So we can only give you 17 episodes." Bill came to me and said, "Those sons of bitches, do you know what they're trying to do?" I said, "Bill, jeez, this'll keep us going all year long. We do those 17 episodes, we keep doing *The Rebel* — it's *great!*" He said [*angrily*], "Look, Andy — *you* make 'em, and I'll *sell* 'em!" So he went back and he said to [ABC executives] Ollie Treyz and Tom Moore, "We don't want 17 episodes, we want 39 episodes!" And they said to him, "Hey! Don't give us that crap. We're gonna give you 17 episodes and next year, we'll pick up *both* series." He said, "No, no, I want 39 episodes *right now!*" They said, "Don't threaten us," and Bill said, "What are you gonna do? Cancel *The Rebel*?!" And they said, "*Don't threaten us.*" So Bill went over to NBC, talked to a guy there named David Levy, showed him the *Yank* pilot, and Levy said, "Tell those guys to go to Hell. *I'll* give you 39 episodes right now." So Bill went back and told them to go to Hell. Then the next week, David Levy was *fired* from NBC [*laughs*]! And the new guys who took over at NBC didn't want to have anything to do with anything that David Levy wanted! And ABC did cancel *The Rebel*! What do you think of *that*? I had two shows on the air *one* day, and the next day I had *none* [*laughs*]!

So that's the short version of what happened. Let me add that I never had two more honest partners in my entire life than Mark Goodson and Bill Todman. Otherwise I would *not* have done *Branded* [the later, Chuck Connors-starring Goodson-Todman Western series]. From the minute we started *The Rebel*, we were in profit, and I received an awful, awful lot of money as my share of the profits. Their bookkeeping was impeccable.

A few years down the road, when Nick found out that I was going to do the series *Hondo* with Ralph Taeger, he came up to my office and he had a couple of eagle claws [left over from *The Rebel*], and he said, "Andy. Here. Give these to Ralph, will ya? And tell him that I wish him good luck." Nick was later in a *Hondo* two-parter, "Hondo and the Apache Kid."

Q: What about Adams' "was-it-suicide-or-murder?" death?

Nick would not destroy himself. Nick was a relatively happy man. He had gone through a divorce, and that was not a good situation. But Nick loved life. I was with him not long before he died, on the set of "Hondo and the Apache Kid," and on that set he was the same old Nick. A doctor had prescribed some kind of medication for him, and it's my theory that Nick took some of this stuff, and when you do, you lose your sense of proportion. I think that he got up in the middle of the night and I think that he just grabbed another bunch of 'em and put 'em in his mouth, and it killed him.

I sure as hell am not ashamed to put my name alongside *The Rebel*. In some ways it was completely different and ahead of its time. I'm not going to say it was a work of art, but it certainly came from the heart.

POSTSCRIPT

Andrew J. Fenady provided for this book a tape recording of comments he made at the memorial service for Rebel *director Irvin Kershner, who died in 2010. (I've transcribed all of it despite a bit of repetition with the interview above.) It begins with Fenady telling the story of their collaboration on KTTV's weekly news-investigative series* Confidential File; *each episode was made up of a 15-minute filmed documentary (made by Fenady and Kershner) followed by newspaper columnist Paul Coates' 15-minute live interview with a person or persons involved with that week's subject.*

I'm Andrew Fenady.

The first words that Irv Kershner ever spoke to me were, "How the hell did you ever get involved in this *mess*?" The mess that he was talking about was a program called *Confidential File*. It was the precursor of *60 Minutes*, looong before there *was* a *60 Minutes*, only we did topics that were a lot more daring and had *never* been [discussed] on television. *Confidential File* was a journey for Kershner and me that lasted more than three years, where we did more than 150 documentaries, working seven days a week, 52 weeks a year. We tackled programs on things that had never been discussed before on television. We did a program on homosexuals — this is in the mid-50s! We did a program on prostitutes, we did a program on LSD, we did a program on venereal disease. The word "syphilis" had never been said before on television. We did a program on capital punishment. I'm the only one who sat down in that chair in San Quentin, one of the two chairs there where 156 people had already been executed; got strapped in and *got up and walked away*. We did programs on rackets, we exposed the used car racket, the television repair racket, the pigeon drop racket, every racket but tennis rackets *[laughs]*! And we did shows on humanity: We did a program on little people (dwarfs and midgets), we did a program on the John Tracy Clinic, we did a program on the Foundation for the Junior Blind when it was bankrupt; they had $37 in the bank and because of *Confidential File* it's still in existence and thriving.

When we finished putting on a program on Sunday night on KTTV, Kersh and I would usually go over to Patsy D'Amore's Villa Capri and sit down with Paul Coates and say, "Okay, where do we stand on the

Fenady and Adams flank Irvin Kershner, who went from directing TV to feature films, including A Fine Madness, The Empire Strikes Back, Never Say Never Again *and* RoboCop 2.

subjects we've been talking about doing? Which one can you get done by next week?" And we would pick a topic and then Kershner and I would start outlining the documentary on Monday, and casting it with wannabe actors who weren't getting paid but they got the exposure, and we would shoot on Tuesday and Wednesday and Thursday, sometimes into Friday. Then Kershner would be over the Movieola patching it together, and I would be over Kershner making notes for the narration. We would go on the air with a work print on Sunday night.

We lived in whorehouses and saloons and the Georgia Street Receiving Hospital, the streets and alleys of Los Angeles. Kershner had a station wagon, a Plymouth that we carried the equipment in, among other things. And it stunk so bad because Kershner smoked the Schimmelpenninck cigars and I smoked any kind of a cigar I could get my hands on, and so we would throw banana peels on the mats to dissipate the odor!

Finally I said, "Kersh, we gotta make one for real."

"What are you talking about?"

"I'm talking about a feature."

He said, "*You bet*. What are we gonna do?"

Well, what did we *know*? We knew kids, we knew the cops, we knew the streets of Los Angeles, we knew dope. We sat down and made an outline for a feature [*Stakeout on Dope Street*], and I made up a budget that nobody could read except me. And then, a true gentleman named Al Kallis took us over to see a fellow named Roger Corman. Now, Roger Corman is a nice man. Roger Corman is a *talented* man. He's an *educated* man. *[With an English accent:]* Oxford, you know! Roger Corman has got allll the money in the world except for a little loose change. But Roger Corman is *cheap*. To say Roger Corman is tight is like saying that Fred Astaire danced a little. But we went over to see him. Now, lately it's been rumored around that Roger produced *Stakeout on Dope Street*. *I'll* tell you what he produced: He produced $15,000. He took a look at the budget, he took a look at the script, and said, "Okay, how much can you make this for?" I said, "We can make it for cash for 21 or 22 thousand." He said *[with impatience]*, "Which *is* it? 21 or 22?" I said, "21! 21! 21!" He said, "I'll give 15,000 for 50 percent of the picture." I asked, "Where are we supposed to get the other six?" He said, "That's *your* problem."

So, Kershner put up two, [cinematographer] Haskell Wexler, who won a couple of Academy Awards later on, put up two, I put up two, and we shot the picture. Yeah, we shot the picture…just like shooting, "The Arabs took the town." I lost 40 pounds: I played the part of a cop, and I had to keep putting sweaters on so you couldn't see how skinny I got. Kershner just about lost his mind; every day there was a problem that we all had to solve. And we cast his arm as the dope addict's arm *[laughs]*: We put a tattoo of dope tracks on there. The picture was shot and Roger didn't see a foot of it until after it was all cut together. An agent named Malcolm Stuart took it over to Warner Brothers, and Jack Warner paid us $150,000 cash, and we thought we were the richest people in the world.

Kershner and I also went under contract to Warners. That lasted six months. Every time we wanted to do something, Warner didn't want to do it, and vice versa. So we went to Paramount. I had written a script called *The Young Captives*, and there was a man there named D.A. Doran, may he rest in peace, and he could green light a picture up to $250,000 if he liked the script. Well, he liked the script and he said, "Boys, how much can you make this for?" I said, "What's the cheapest picture you made in the last coupla years, D.A.?" He said, "$220,000." We said, "We'll do it for 210." *And we did.*

There was a fella named Nick Adams. Very nice guy, very talented man. I met him when we were working out at a gymnasium. He kept saying, "Andy, Andy! Write me a series. I wanna do a series." I said, "Well, what do you want to do?" He said *[imitating James Cagney]*, "I do a great Jimmy Cagney. How 'bout like a *Johnny Come Lately*?" I said, "No." "I do Cary Grant!" "No, no, no!" *[laughs]* At that time, out of the ten top shows on television, eight were Westerns, and I said, "Fellas, we're going to do a Western." Kershner said to me, "Andy...I have never directed a Western." I said, "Kersh...I have never *written* a Western." *But* — I wrote it, he directed it, and the odds against our selling that pilot were thousands to one because we were competing with MCA, William Morris, Four Star, *all* of them. But I'll never forget, we were sitting in the projection room at Paramount, Kershner, my brother Georg, Nick Adams and Dan Blocker, watching a picture called *Sunset Blvd.* [1950]. The phone rang and it was Harris Katleman, who worked over at Goodson-Todman. He said, "Andy, Andy, the greatest news in the world! Are you ready for *this*?: We *made* it, the pilot sold!" I said, "Harris, we'll call you back. We're right in the middle of the monkey scene in *Sunset Blvd.*" *[laughs]* So that's how that happened! After Kershner directed a bunch of episodes, he got the opportunity to direct *The Hoodlum Priest* [1961] with Don Murray. Kersh came to me and he said, "Andy, what do you think? What should I do? You want me to stay?" I said, "Kersh, don't be silly. This is a *great* opportunity. You go 'head and *do* it. And give 'em hell. We'll *always* be partners, we'll *always* be pals. Go ahead." So he did.

I won't make a miniseries out of this, I've probably talked too long anyhow, but...no matter where Kersh and I met for the next 50 years, no matter how or when, no matter what the circumstances, we'd always throw our arms around each other, we'd always hug each other and, yes, we'd always kiss each other.

The last line that David Niven spoke to Ronald Colman in a picture called *The Prisoner of Zenda* [1937] was, "Fate doesn't always make the right men kings." That's true. But Fate *does*, sometimes, make the right men *partners* and *pals*. So I'll just say, "Kersh...so long, partner. So long, pal. See you on location."

Pat Fielder
WRITES *THE RIFLEMAN*

His modified Winchester at the ready, Chuck Connors starred in Levy–Gardner–Laven's 1958-63 teleseries The Rifleman. *Pat Fielder scripted over a half-dozen episodes.*

Pasadena-born Pat Fielder was working as a production assistant-story editor-secretary at Levy-Gardner-Laven when her bosses offered her a chance to write her first screenplay, The Monster That Challenged the World *(1957). Scripts for more sci-fi and horror movies followed, and then writing chores on one of L-G-L's first TV series,* The Rifleman. *Here Fielder (still writing away in the 21st century) recalls her days on that Chuck Connors-Johnny Crawford-starring series and on L-G-L's feature* Geronimo *(1962), with Connors in the title role.*

PAT FIELDER: Jules Levy, Arthur Gardner and Arnold Laven were absolutely terrific, they were wonderful. They really were my "family," they protected me, they were so good. Jules Levy was the one who had the oddball ideas — ideas from "out in left field." He was the one who thought up wild things to do. Jules and Arnold Laven had both been script supervisors [prior to the 1951 formation of L-G-L] and they had learned all aspects of set operations. Arnold wanted to be a director and so he became a director, and Jules always wanted to be a producer and so he became a producer. Arthur Gardner had been a production manager and wanted to be a producer. It was not the Hollywood scene at all, they were just really great, wonderful guys. Honest guys, and so hard-working.

Their first picture was called *Without Warning!* [1952]. It was shot in black-and-white on the streets of LA, natural locations, and they made it very cheaply. I first worked for them in 1952 when they made *Vice Squad.* I was just out of school, broke and out of work, and I was asked by a friend to take on a two-week typing job that she was unable to do. So I went to work for L-G-L and met them for the first time and typed their script of *Vice Squad,* and they asked me to stay on during the shooting.

The way *The Rifleman* came about was, Levy-Gardner-Laven made an arrangement with Chuck Connors: The way they were able to get him for a television series was by promising him a theatrical role, which they did give him when he later starred for them in the movie *Geronimo,* which I wrote. On *The Rifleman,* I was one of several writers. I wrote seven of them, but Sam Peckinpah wrote the pilot ["The Sharpshooter"]. Now, I don't think it was Sam who came up with the *idea* for the series, I think it was Arthur, Arnold and Jules, and then they brought Sam in. Sam wrote a number of *Rifleman*s and he also directed several. That was the point at which Sam was trying to make his move into directing. Sam was a great character, a sweetheart, and became a good friend of mine. He was a very, very unusual but *loyal* person, he really was. And very creative. I was reading one of his *Rifleman* scripts the other day, and only a country boy could have written it: It was so full of the things that he actually knew, because he grew up in Fresno and he knew the country, he hunted and he rode and he did all those things, so when he *wrote* about them, there was a great reality about them.

Sam was *so* individual, such an unusual person. And he was a scholar. At that time he lived in a huge Quonset hut above Malibu, he and his wife and their coupla kids, and the place was wiped out in one of those Malibu fires. Sam said he had *10,000* books in this domicile, that were all burned to a crisp. He was brokenhearted over that! I was divorced, and he felt sorry for me because he was a pal, so he introduced me to his *best friend [laughs]* — *those* kinds of things happened too. He was a man in charge, that's the best way I can describe Sam! Sometimes he was blunt and difficult and hard to get along with, but generally he knew what he wanted and he was very much devoted to getting that result.

Chuck Connors was an interesting guy. He was very restless at the time; he had been a baseball player and had had that career as an athlete, and then he made the transition into acting, and he was a really nice, down-to-earth kind of guy. By the time we were on location in Mexico on *Geronimo*, he was divorced from his wife and he met Kamala Devi, his leading lady, whom he later married. Kamala was a beautiful Indian girl — an Indian-from-India girl. They made a great couple. We were in Durango for three months shooting *Geronimo*, so we all became very, very close.

Levy-Gardner-Laven mostly had men writing the *Rifleman* scripts. I wrote several things that were kinda from a woman's point of view, and therefore *unusual* in the West at the time. I think it was an interesting transition to a kind-of "softer" touch. Maggie Armen, who also wrote for L-G-L, scripted some *Rifleman*s and she did some *Big Valley*s, and she and I became great friends. I'm now working with her son David on an adaptation of a novel that Maggie wrote called *The Hanging of Father Miguel* — we've written a screenplay on it. We all stay kind of interconnected, because it was a very close group of people who were doing most of the writing at L-G-L at the time. We all knew each other and were friends and stayed up all night writing. Because there was always a terrible deadline facing you! It was always hard to get the script in on time, but you *had* to do it or…get shot *[laughs]!*

Levy, Gardner and Laven spent an awful lot of time trying to develop the right kind of stories. I think that's why the series was such a success; they really put all their effort into it, and they did a terrific job. *The*

Rifleman was shot at CBS Studio Center, that little studio [formerly Republic] off of Ventura Boulevard near Laurel Canyon. L-G-L had a suite of offices there, and I had an office; L-G-L had two or three writers whom they had given offices to, working on the various series. The *Rifleman* soundstage had the downtown North Fork, the bar and the various stores and Sheriff Micah's office and so on. There was dirt all over the

North Fork, New Mexico, homesteader Lucas McCain (Connors) and his young son Mark (Johnny Crawford), The Rifleman's *leading characters.*

floor and they'd bring horses in and they'd shoot all the ride-ins on this big soundstage. I was free to go over and hang out on the set any time I wanted to. There was no objection to a writer being on the set, which I thought was really miraculous and wonderful, because we were all sort of "part of the team." Of course, you could *not* go up to the director and say, "Why did you change that line?" *[laughs]* — you wouldn't do *that*, because if you *did*, you wouldn't be on the set very much longer! But, no, we were always welcome. Arnold Laven directed a lot of the shows, and Sam Peckinpah did a couple, and Paul Landres and so on. Some of my episodes were "The Woman" with Patricia Barry [as a suffragette] and "Meeting at Midnight," a vigilante story, and "Blood Brother," about a blood transfusion. I re-read "The Princess" the other day, and it was a sweet script — a "runaway royal family members" story, with the kids put up in Lucas McCain's house before deciding to go back to their royal duties in Europe. I did "The Grasshopper" about robbers on a train, and the train being stopped by an invasion of grasshoppers, and I wrote a pilot which was done on *The Rifleman*, called "The Lariat," with Dick Anderson, but they never got it sold into a series. My favorite title [out of her episodes] was "One Went to Denver." Do you know the Western song with the lyrics "One went to Denver, the other went wrong"? I always loved that song! We did a lot of historical research and we looked into the West very carefully, trying to figure out what the proper stories would be. We were into medicine ["Blood Brothers"] and all kinds of things.

Jules was elated that he and Arthur were able to acquire the title *Geronimo* from the MPAA Registration Service. He asked me if I knew anything about the famous Indian rebel. Of course I *didn't*, but I said I'd begin research and I could learn. I wrote a *very* long one-line outline and finally got approval to write the screenplay. Once I finished it and United Artists was happy with it, we got a commitment to shoot it. It was agreed that I would be the dialogue director and go with the company to location to Durango, Mexico. I traveled with [director] Arnold Laven to scout the locations and draw his camera setups as well as adjust what dialogue was necessary, coach the actors, etc. We were on location, counting pre-production time, for about three to four months. *Geronimo* was shot at some point when *The Rifleman* went on hiatus. It was a very, very happy shoot. Arnold of course was there because he directed it, and Arthur and Jules were on the set too. Because Chuck Connors had bright blue eyes [inappropriate for the role], he was going to wear brown contact lenses; however, we had a lot of wind and dust blowing on the set, because we were way out in the mountain country, and so he wasn't able to wear them and eventually they had to give up the contact lens idea. At one point I tried to compensate by writing a new line for one of the cavalrymen, asking Geronimo if he was a Yaqui, because I knew that Yaquis had blue eyes *[laughs]!* But they didn't use that line, it was cut.

Q: Geronimo *had some excellent parts for women — from Kamala Devi's character to the farm woman who brings the Indians into her house for a chicken dinner.*

Well, women had not really been dealt with particularly in Westerns in that sense. And certainly not Indian women. I loved *Geronimo,* and I wish I could have gone even further with it. But we had to adhere to certain action. The true story of the Indians and the reservations is really a tragic story. The Indians weren't treated fairly. They were caged, in that sense, put on reservations and forced to be farmers, and I felt a great deal of sympathy for that.

Pat Fielder in a recent shot.

I finally left Levy-Gardner-Laven because I felt a need to expand my horizons and move away from "the family" [the L-G-L "family"]. There was a great freelance market for television at that time, something that doesn't exist today. I wrote for medical shows, legal shows, cop shows, psychiatric shows, all that kind of thing. And I wrote a lot of Westerns — *The Rebel, Wagon Train, The Road West, The High Chaparral, Alias Smith and Jones, Law of the Plainsman* and many others, and that's a whole bunch!

When I think back on *The Rifleman,* they're all really good memories. I had mixed feelings about leaving Levy-Gardner-Laven because I was so close to them but, as I mentioned, I felt that I needed to widen my scope. And yet sometimes I thought, "Maybe I *should* have stuck around," 'cause they were such good guys. It was a big, important part of my life.

Beryl Braithwaite Hart

WHEN HAWKEYE MET PIE-EYED…

The way Beryl Braithwaite tells it, Lon Chaney Jr. (left) was a light drinker: As soon as it got light, he started drinking!

Actress Beryl Braithwaite isn't known for Westerns, but the one Western TV appearance she did make changed her life: Guesting on an episode of the Canadian-made Hawkeye and the Last of the Mohicans, *she met and fell for its star John Hart — and vice versa — and they married just days later. Best man at their wedding: series co-star Lon Chaney, Jr., the perennially plastered performer who played Hawkeye's redskin sidekick Chingachgook. Beryl Hart, widowed since 2009, here ruefully recalls various run-ins with the actor who put the "hic" in* Mohicans...

BERYL BRAITHWAITE: I first met Lon Chaney, Jr., when I was on the set of *Hawkeye and the Last of the Mohicans* as an actress. I was playing a settler's wife who was arriving with consumption, and in one exterior scene they told me to cough. When I coughed, I coughed so that "it could be heard in the back of the theater," if you know what I mean, and both John and Lon tumbled out of Lon's camper, thinking that somebody was dying! John and I were married about ten days later [on Friday, February 22, 1957]. I was 20, he was 39. Lon was the best man.

The wedding took place at Lorne Park Methodist in Mississauga at eight o'clock at night. John had to drive through a snowstorm to get to the church, and on the way he kept saying to Lon, "Do you have the ring?" And Lon would say, in a drunken voice, "I have the ring." But he'd never show it to John or pat his pocket or *any*thing, to ease John's mind that he really *did* have it. When John got to the church, he went up to the minister and said, "I don't know whether this guy has the ring or not." And the minister said, "I *always* bring a spare." Well, it turned out Lon *did* have the ring.

At the reception at the Royal York Hotel, Lon was pretty well lit. I had a little brother who was there, three years old, almost four, and at one point Lon tried to pick Colin up by the *ears*. And Colin gave him a swift kick in the shins *[laughs]!*

Everybody was toasting the bride. These were all my friends, because John (being from California) didn't have many people at the wedding other than some of the *Hawkeye* crew. It was a very small wedding, as you can imagine. Lon stood up and he was going to make a toast to John, and he said *[slurring]*, "John Hart has brought something to Canada..." And then he looked around at all these faces, and he said, "...that Canada can *well afford.*" And sat down *[laughs]!* He realized he'd made *some* sort of a gaffe! I come from a theatrical family, and all the participants at the reception were writers and actors and so on. I think they thought [Chaney's antics] were hilarious. They certainly weren't upset in any way.

Lon really wanted to do everything a best man's supposed to do, so he had called Patsy, his wife, to find out what a best man did. And, boy, he *did* it, and turned into a pain in the neck, really, because he'd had so much to drink. For instance, the Royal York Hotel has a tunnel that runs underground, under a street, to a railway station, and as John and I were leaving for the station, Lon came along too, carrying our luggage, two or

Rapids transit!: John Hart (right) as Hawkeye and Lon Chaney, Jr., as his blood brother Chingachgook braved the "Eastern frontier" in the syndicated teleseries Hawkeye and the Last of the Mohicans.

three bags, and he was hustling some of the other guests to go through the tunnel to the station with us. John was tired and was getting a little put-out with all of this. Then at the station, Lon had confetti which he proceeded to throw, and John didn't want *any* part of that and he got very perturbed and he just about lost it. But John and I finally got on the train and took off.

I do have to say, however, that Lon was *extremely* courteous to John's mother Enid, who arrived from California just before the wedding. For our honeymoon, all John and I could do was go away for the weekend, to Montreal; we had to be back on Sunday afternoon because John had to be on the *Hawkeye* set on Monday morning. And Lon took great care of Enid while we were away: He didn't drink a lot, he cooked her dinner, he took her out and he was very gracious. Lon was a *heck* of a good cook. He made John and me some wonderful dinners up there in Canada.

Q: Did you ever meet Patsy, Lon's wife?

I never saw Patsy except one time. After John and I got married, we were there in Toronto for another six weeks before the series was over, and I think it must have been during those six weeks.

Lon really drank too much. He drank a fifth by noon, and a fifth by five, and a fifth by bedtime. And so on *Hawkeye* they tried to do all his lines, etc., in the morning. He was a good actor — if they *did* it in the morning! When *Hawkeye* was shooting, John and I lived in an apartment house, about a 20-story apartment house, right on the shore of Lake Ontario, and Lon lived one floor up from us. This is the way every morning of our married life started out: The first thing John would do when he got up at 4:30 was unlock the door, and then some time later, after I'd had made John his breakfast, Lon would come down and knock, open the door and get a good swig from John's bottle of Jim Beam, which John would leave on the kitchen counter. God, first thing in the morning! That would be Lon's first drink of the day, every day. Well, no, it probably *wasn't* the first *[laughs]!*

John and Lon couldn't go to professional hockey games because they were played at night and went too late, so they took to going to the Sunday afternoon hockey games, which was the Senior A. Frank Mahovlich was playing then, a lot of guys who later became big stars. Lon would carry a bottle to the hockey games, and he'd be pretty far gone. They certainly did not allow liquor at the hockey games, but what could you do with Lon *[laughs]*?

After the series was over, John and I moved to Southern California, and Lon would call occasionally. And sometimes, when you could tell he'd been drinking, he would call and he would want John to go hunting with him. Well, John had given up hunting years before, and was now pretty *anti*-hunting. But finally John said to me, "Lon lives in this place called Warner Springs and I think we should go down and see his ranch and spend the night." So we trundled down. I think this would have been the early 1960s; there was no freeway then, so it was a heckuva long way.

Lon's ranch was a *really* nice place, with all the bedrooms opening off a big central room. Well, Lon was drunk when we got there — and when Lon got drunk, he got very aggressive and abusive. He was determined that he and John were going to go out and shoot a deer. And John was determined he *wasn't* going to go out and shoot a deer. Unfortunately, that sorta set the tone for the evening. Then whatever Lon was cooking burned; he'd had so much to drink that he forgot it, and it burned, and that made him even angrier. Finally it got pretty nasty, with Lon threatening to start a fight. He would never have hit me or harmed me in any way…I don't think…but John wanted me out of there; he said to me, "You go in the guest bedroom, and I'll take care of this. Lock the door if you can, or put a chair under the knob…" I was *very* glad to get out of there, because Lon was ranting and raving and not making any sense.

I never knew what happened between them after I went to bed, but I don't think it ever came to a physical confrontation. I fell asleep, John came to bed, and we got out of there the next morning.

Q: You didn't ask John, the next morning, what else had happened?

No. In the morning, Lon was in a drunken stupor and we left.

Q: Was Patsy there?

When John and I visited Lon at his ranch, Patsy was not there. She had had a *loooong* association with Lon, and I think she had figured out that the best way for them to co-exist was to stay apart. That was my impression anyway. By the time of our visit, she lived somewhere other than the ranch, down by the ocean somewhere. I think Lon had passed out of her life a long time before he passed away.

That visit at the ranch was the last time I ever saw Lon. When we left that day, I was so glad to leave, and I swore I would never come down to those mountains again no matter *what*. But the codicil to that story is that John and I later *moved* there, and lived for 17 years about three miles from the Chaney ranch. It was still there, and other people owned it, and they talked about digging up *quantities* of bottles. For some reason, Lon had buried them all around the house! I could never make myself go down and see that ranch again, I couldn't go *that* far.

Wedding daze! John Hart's mother Enid, Chaney, newlyweds Beryl and Hart, and Beryl's sister Shari pose for a picture at Lorne Park Methodist. Fourteen-year-old Shari, Beryl's only attendant, and Chaney signed the marriage certificate.

Thinking back, I don't know how Lon would have gotten through that *Hawkeye* series without John, I really don't. And John was no saint — but he sure didn't drink as much as Lon. John would jolly Lon along in the afternoons, when there were scenes still to be done and Lon was getting a little argumentative. With a TV series, it's important to keep going and stay on schedule. I think everybody [on the *Hawkeye* series] appreciated what John did, because Lon was big and powerful and nobody wanted to deal with an angry Lon. So John did his bit.

Richard Kline

MEMORIES OF
CHARLES STARRETT

Richard Kline operating a camera on The Wackiest Ship in the Army?
(1960).

Long before Richard Kline photographed movies on the level of Camelot, Star Trek: The Motion Picture, Body Heat, Hang 'em High *and* The Andromeda Strain, *he learned his trade via years of uncredited work as assistant cameraman and camera operator on pictures both major and minor. The son of cinematographer Benjamin H. Kline, Richard began at Columbia in 1943 as a 16-year-old, and some of the movies on which he worked in those early years were the low-budget Westerns of cowboy star Charles Starrett.*

RICHARD KLINE: Charlie Starrett was always a very decent person. He averaged eight Westerns a year for Columbia, and those pictures were eight days apiece, so every year he worked 64 days. As I recall, he was paid $64,000 a year for those Westerns, so...a thousand dollars a day. And yet, according to Charlie, nobody knew who he was; he could go to, say, the market and nobody would recognize him. He was happy about that, he said, "I don't *want* to be hounded!"

He was from the Starrett family, the tool family out of the East Coast; that company's still in business [the L.S. Starrett Company, headquartered in Athol, Massachusetts, Charles' birthplace]. You could tell he was from Massachusetts, he'd say "hoss" instead of horse *[laughs]*. Actually, his elocution wasn't the best, he was a little bit of a mush-mouth — he sometimes mumbled when he spoke, and was kind of hard to understand. Directors occasionally had to go several takes as he cleaned up his speech pattern. Charlie went to Dartmouth, played football there, and then got into the acting. I don't know how he was chosen [to star in Westerns] but it had to have been his looks. I'm certain that *some*body, once they saw him, said, "He'd make a great Western star," 'cause he "looked the part," he was like Gary Cooper and some of the other great stars who actually *looked* Western. Charlie really was a good-looking guy, *so* "Western-looking," six foot four, and he had a big head that really filled out that hat. And a lovely, fun guy. I don't think he considered him*self* a great actor but he tried hard, he put in a good effort.

When we worked on those Starrett pictures, working out at one of the movie ranches, we put in a full day. At 5:30 or 6 in the morning, we would leave from Columbia Pictures on Gower and Sunset on a bus, or we might have *two* busses sometimes. Each bus could hold about 35 people. The busses were for the crew, and extras would also be on the bus, people like that. The members of the cast would go out independently in "stretch-outs," conventional cars that the studio supplied. And Charlie always got there in his *own* car. This was when station wagons were just coming in, and he had one of the very first Cadillac station wagons. The Cadillac was the cream of the crop, and he was so proud of that!

Also, the bus would pick up people on the way; they'd be sitting on the curb along Ventura Blvd., different extras and so on. It was really funny: We were in kind of "a world of our own" making those pictures. No matter what else was happening in the world, nothing bothered those pictures! It would take an hour to get to one of the two ranches we worked at, Corrigan Ranch or Iverson's Ranch, which were about 10, 15 minutes away from each other. We'd work at one or the other, or maybe sometimes we'd work at *both* in a given day. The production people were experts at planning each day: We'd work in the flats during the day, doing at least 60, 70 set-ups, maybe as much as a hundred, which is a *lot* by today's standards. In summertime, it was really hot there, and in the winter, it could be very cold! They tried to shoot these Westerns in the spring and summer, when the weather was more favorable, but this was barren, wild country. We'd work through the day, first on the flats, and the production people planned it so that generally we would wind up, at the end of the day, working on a higher level. Both ranches had an area that we called Panic Peak and we'd end up there, where the sun lasted the longest, and finish our day's work. Then we'd wrap quickly and start heading back to the studio. There was a little more traffic coming back, so we'd get back to Columbia in darkness, 7, 7:30. They were long days.

[Directing-wise] there was no playing around with drama. That was true of Ray Nazarro particularly: He had only one bit of direction he gave to everybody, he'd say, "Okay, roll 'em. *Nice and bright.*" He'd always say "Nice and bright," that's all the direction there was. No matter *what* the scene was, he asked for "nice and bright"! And if we didn't get through the whole [planned shot], whenever Ray could he would say, "All right, cut. Let's pick it up from…" [rather than starting from the beginning again]. Ray was the brother of the famous Cliff Nazarro, a double-talker, very well-known on radio — and Ray was a very fast talker himself! He was an assistant director originally, so he had a very good production background and knew the fundamentals of filmmaking. Also, he knew that these Starrett pictures were not works of art — they were not "drama," put it that way!

Jack Fier [who worked on Starrett Westerns as a production manager and as a producer] eventually became the head of production at Columbia, overseeing all pictures. Fier — the name implied exactly what he was [*laughs*]! A heart of gold but, boy, was he rough, and he called things as they were, or as he thought it should be. But he was always decent on these Westerns. He and Colbert Clark [another producer] were different types of people. Colbert was a very easygoing guy, you hardly knew he was around.

The other workers that I remember are mainly the stunt people. They were rough'n'tough, boy, they did a lot of falls off horses and that type of thing. One was Richard Farnsworth, who became a pretty good actor

Composite photo of Charles Starrett alongside his alter ego, the masked do-gooder The Durango Kid. Cameraman Richard Kline guesses that Starrett began getting Western roles simply because he "actually looked Western."

in his elder years. He had a bad shoulder and on those Starretts, he used to throw it out of the socket all the time, by falling off a horse, generally. They'd have to take him to the hospital and put it back in! (This was long before they had first aid men and ambulances on the locations, so if somebody hurt themselves, they'd be taken to the closest hospital in a car.) Then there was another real rough'n'tumble guy, Bob Cason. Ted Mapes was also a stuntman for Charlie, but when I first met him, he really wasn't doing stunt work, I only knew him as an SAG type, doing a lot of extra work and bit parts at Columbia — they liked him a lot. He'd been a grip before he was an actor. Real nice man, tall and lanky, he looked very Western, and had great character in his face.

Right after the war, Jocko Mahoney became Charlie Starrett's main double. Jocko was a very good gymnast, a swimmer, played football, really a terrific athlete. He ended up with a heart attack — he abused himself pretty well. There was another stuntman who worked in that Starrett group, Al Wyatt. I think Al was responsible for Jocko becoming such a terrific horseman. These were terrific guys. Well, *every*body was — these were sensational people to be around. Colorful, bold, they'd play gags on each other, they really had a lot of fun. The wranglers, whose names I've forgotten now, they were tough too. In the sun all day long on their horses, maintaining the horses and that type of thing. It was tough work, rough work, but these were dedicated, rugged people. And they, too, looked the part, they really looked Western.

Ace Hudkins was a well-known ex-fighter, a middleweight boxer, and he and his brother Clyde supplied all the horses for these movies except for the lead horses. Ralph McCutcheon trained and took care of the lead horses, whereas Ace took care of the atmosphere horses. Ace was *another* rough'n'tumble guy. Years earlier, he had been shot in some kind of an altercation, and he *lived*, obviously, but it affected his liver or his kidneys, and when it was cold, like in the mornings, he was totally blue! He looked like a Picasso painting from the Blue Period *[laughs]* — amazing! Then as it'd warm up, he was *less* blue. As we made these pictures, Hudkins also was kind of head of the gambling consortium. They gambled all day long, particularly at lunchtime. Crap games, card games, things like that. Anybody not working at a particular time was gambling! I've never been a gambler, I didn't take part.

They didn't have honey wagons then, so if you had to go, you went behind a tree or something. When somebody had to go, the prop men would say, "Go behind that tree over there" or "Go behind that brush" or whatever. Well, these prop men were really gagsters: They'd set up a very convenient place for somebody to go take a dump or whatever, and they had a shovel with a long, long, long handle on it. As the guy ["did his business"], the prop men, hiding nearby, would catch it in the shovel and then quietly pull it away. The person who [just took a dump] would stand up and turn around, and there'd be nothing there *[laughs]!* It surprised a lot of people! There were gags like that all the time — unbelievable!

Another composite shot with an unmasked Starrett in the inset, and astride a horse as The Durango Kid. *Mounting horses was a challenge for the actor, according to Kline; "He just wasn't really well-coordinated."*

Charlie always had problems around a horse. Horses have "horse sense" and they knew he was afraid of 'em! So he bought his own horse and Ralph McCutcheon began training it. And when the new horse was ready, the day we used it for the first time, Charlie walked behind the horse and the horse kicked him in the balls *[laughs]*, and we had to shut down for a few days. If you saw that happen in a movie about a Western star, you wouldn't believe it, but it really happened. He got rid of the horse right away! Also, Charlie was not the best-coordinated guy in the world. He would trip on his own spurs and that type of thing. I hate to use the word "clumsy," but...he just wasn't really well-coordinated. When Ray Nazarro would be setting up a shot in which Charlie was going to get on his horse, when he would say, "Okay, Charlie, you mount the horse here," somebody'd always say, "Get a two-step ready." A two-step was, like, two apple boxes put together, and it'd be out of frame, and as Charlie mounted, he could step up onto that in order to look better getting onto the horse. The camera and sound guys had a pool, betting on how many takes it would take for Charlie to get on his horse in a decent [usable in the movie] way. As I mentioned earlier, there was a lot of gambling on those sets, the crap games and card games, and also all kinds of pools, for football and so on. Once when we were having one of our pools betting on how many takes it'd take for Charlie to get on the horse, Charlie overheard one of the camera or sound guys say, "Count me in!"; Charlie realized we were starting a pool, and he said, "Count *me* in, too!" He didn't realize that we were betting on *him [laughs]!*

Charlie, yes, he had the mush mouth and he wasn't the most coordinated guy in the world, but he was a *good* guy, very cooperative, tried hard, and he ended up number five on one of the lists of the top cowboy stars. He was the father of twin boys that he talked about often, he was very fond of them.

The guys who made these pictures were just fun people who loved to gamble; who loved to be gagsters; they drank pretty good too; and they loved the hard work. "Hard work" is not a negative, it *can* be fun. And it really *was* in this case. I was very lucky to work in that environment.

June Lockhart
TV WESTERN WOMAN

Gene Lockhart and his wife Kathleen, joined by their 13-year-old daughter June (left) and Terry Kilburn, played the Cratchit family in the MGM version of A Christmas Carol *(1938).*

June Lockhart — Western woman? This TV legend is so well-known for Lassie *and other modern-day mom roles (and futuristic mom roles — remember* Lost in Space?*) that it's easy to forget that, in the days when cowboys and marshals and drovers dominated the TV range seven days a week, she guested in several of the top series — and adored the experience. With great excitement over finally being asked about this aspect of her nearly lifelong career, June Lockhart relives her Western memories...*

JUNE LOCKHART: As a kid, I loved Westerns, and I was a big fan of John Wayne's. I remember [as a teenager] seeing him in *Tall in the Saddle* [1944] at Grauman's Chinese or some Hollywood Boulevard movie theater, and thinking that he was pretty hot! I never worked with him but I met him once on a flight back from Hawaii, where we were seatmates. He was a great person to travel with 'cause he didn't talk *[laughs]*. Well, *you* know, you don't want somebody bending your ear for all that time!

I treasure my experiences with Westerns. First of all, I love doing work in period costumes, and so to be in Westerns with long clothes and the petticoats and the waist cinch and the big, heavy boots and the whole thing — glorious! The *period* appealed to me so much. *Have Gun — Will Travel* may have been my first. I played a lady doctor, Phyllis Thackeray, in two episodes, and I cured everybody of small pox in one of 'em! They were both good scripts and it was a very interesting role. Richard Boone was nice to work with. He and I had the same agent, so there was a little "connection" there, but I had never met him before we did the first show. He played Paladin in that show with great authority. In one of the episodes ["No Visitors," 1957], I had to ride a horse, and I'm not a horsewoman, I had never ridden much. He and I were to ride off across a field. Well, my foot came out of the stirrup, and I knew I had no control over this beast at all. We got out of camera range and we went for what seemed a *very* long time to me, at slow gallop, until he reached over and grabbed the reins and reined the horse in for me. Which was very nice, because otherwise I would still be out there riding, hanging on *[laughs]*. Speaking about a horse running away with its rider, when my father Gene Lockhart was doing *Billy the Kid* [1941], playing the evil cattle baron, *his* horse ran away with him. Daddy didn't ride either, and when this happened, the director turned to the cameraman and put his head down — he couldn't watch — and he said, "Lemme know when it happens" [when Gene falls off the horse]. But I guess somebody came and reined *him* in, too. When I see *Billy the Kid*, I know exactly the shot where he's about to go off into the horizon, his horse just galloping away!

Also in that *Have Gun – Will Travel*, Boone and I had a rather intimate scene as the sun was setting. It was quite a provocative scene, but of course in those days you didn't get to touch all that much or really do *any*thing, 'cause the children were watching. So we did the long shot, and then he had to leave for some reason. And so my closeup was done with the script supervisor — a *lady!* Here I was playing this intimate love scene

This page, facing page: Lockhart shared some heroics (and got romantic) with Richard Boone in the two Have Gun – Will Travel *episodes in which she played physician Phyllis Thackeray, "No Visitors" (1957) and "The Return of Dr. Thackeray" (1958).*

with this woman, which was a first for me *[laughs]*. I never had done a love scene with a leading man who was played by a woman, because the leading man had gotten in his car and gone home! This was an exterior, out in Simi Valley, which is now all housing and RVs for sale. On all these Westerns that I did, we were out on location in the dust and dirt of the San Fernando Valley, where we'd have to arrive really early in the

morning, before the sun rises. It just always appealed to my imagination, I loved the sets and the whole atmosphere of doing a Western.

I had a very nice time working with Boone. I've heard that later he became very difficult [became a drinker] but during the *Have Gun – Will Travel* time he was very disciplined, and he was slim, keeping himself in good shape. And then, when he went on to do the other things [drink], he was less than disciplined, and very large and fat.

Q: He had that pockmarked face, perfect for a villain — but I guess he was attractive to some women.] Yes, wasn't that strange? Apparently he had an appeal for some women who liked the feeling of…maybe…a little *threat?*

I did a *Cimarron City* with George Montgomery but the one I really remember from that is Audrey Totter. She was a gem, oh my God what a wonderful woman. In one scene she had been raped or attacked or something, and was lying in a barn on hay. As we were all standing around, I leaned over her and I said, "You know, you got this part 'cause they knew you were good in the hay." *[laughs]* That held everything up for about four minutes! She was just a great dame, the kind of actress you'd love to work with in a loooong run, because she was solid and "there" and fun and very creative and a professional. I really enjoyed Audrey very much and had great respect for her.

James Arness [*Gunsmoke*] was absolutely marvelous, and extreee-eemely tall. I played a woman named Crazy Beulah, an alco-holic murderous crazy person — I shot Wayne Morris! Oh, and I was also a hooker *[laughs]*. But by the end, I was *sorry*. All within 25 minutes! That was a nifty part, and I've got some stills of that with me clutching a bottle, with my cleavage showing and my hair down. Wonderful! Sam Peckin-pah wrote it — can you imagine? Again, James Arness was like 9'9" *[laughs]*, he looked like he had to be the tallest man in the world, and when you worked with him, you had to always stand up on a little platform so that your face could be in the shot with him. I'm 5'5", and so there *he* was, very very tall. Even standing on the platform, my face was still only level with his belly. We were playing this scene, very dramatic, heavy stuff, at about 12:30, 12:40 in the afternoon, just before we were scheduled to break for lunch. Well, his stomach rumbled in the middle of the scene! It was like a kettledrum, so loud that everybody could hear it. *[In a "grand lady" tone of voice:]* But I, being professional, went right on with the dialogue, and he being the pro that *he* was, answered me back. But then it rumbled *again*. Well, this time I couldn't hold in it, I started to giggle, and with the camera still running, I looked directly at his belly. I lowered my gaze into his stomach area, at his ribcage, where this loud, rumbling noise had come from, and we *all* broke up. And *he* chuckled too.

I had worked with Ward Bond in New York, on the live *Pulitzer Prize Playhouse*, so when I did *Wagon Train* I knew him already — and

One of the actress' favorite Western parts was as the unstable Beulah in the 1958 Gunsmoke *episode "Dirt," co-scripted by Sam Peckinpah.*

I also knew Bob Horton. One of the two episodes I did was good, very interesting: I was raped by an Indian and gave birth to the baby, and my husband didn't want anything more to do with me because I'd had that terrible experience. That was rather a heavy plot *[laughs]!* They had a real live, little teeny baby, wrapped in a blanket, for me to hold while I was sitting in the back of a wagon. It was such a young baby, it turned its little head towards my breast *[laughs]!* It recognized the feeling of the arms around it and turned and I thought, "*Whoa*, wait a minute!" Everybody laughed at that, and they had to cut.

Ward Bond and Bob Horton were grand guys, and also James Gregory who played my husband. Ward was very right-wing, that was a constant in his life, so you didn't bring it up if you didn't want to hear a lecture. When we were doing the *Pulitzer Prize Playhouse* in New York, that was in the middle of all the McCarthy hearings, so [his attitude] was far more "present." Ward was...*stolid,* let me put it that way. I'm trying to give you a variety of adjectives for these people [rather than] "He was great" and "He was fine" and "He was nice." I'm kinda vain about my vocabulary so I hope I'm giving you some variety here, and "stolid" would be the word for Ward Bond!

Rawhide was grand, because that was the pilot and it was very, very good. *Rawhide* was Clint Eastwood's "big break." I remember walking down one of the Western streets with Clint (I had watched him work in a couple of scenes, and I'd already played a couple of scenes with him), and I said, "Clint, you'll be a big star. You've got it. You're a good actor and you have the quality which I *know* will make you a great success." And he looked at me and he said, "Ya *think* so?" and I said, "Oh my, yes." Because Clint had tremendous concentration and, in addition to whatever lines he was saying and what scene he was playing, he worked as though he had a *secret.* There *are* some actors like that, who always work as though they have a subtext. He had that quality. I always remember him with great admiration.

Branded was a pilot again — and there's *another* tall man, Chuck Connors. In the story, which was "setting things up" for the series, his character [an ex-soldier wrongly accused of cowardice] came to me because I had letters from my late soldier-husband that would help clear him. Chuck was a neat guy. *All* of these guys had a wonderful kind of simple honesty about them, and about their work. There was no affectation; there was a nice, simplistic thing about the way they played, which was easy to work with. Often the other roles [each episode's guest stars] were the ones who carried all the emotion, the tears, the carrying-on, the drama, while these guys were the steady, true leading men — and this was often so in their real lives. With each of these men that we have mentioned, they knew their lines, they came prepared. I think they nearly all smoked — and they're nearly all *gone*.

On *Death Valley Days* I played the real-life character Ina Coolbrith, the first Poet Laureate of an American state. Kathy Garver was in it playing a ballet dancer named Dorita Duncan, a name close to that of Isadora Duncan, the [real-life] ballet dancer who died when she got her beauti-

ful long scarf caught in the rear wheel of the convertible in which she was riding in France. (And it became kind of a joke: "My God, that scarf is as long as Isadora Duncan's, don't step on it!") My poet befriends Kathy's ballet dancer and encourages her in the dancing. One nice thing about that episode was, they needed some children in it, and so they let my two daughters Junie and Annie play two of the little girls, which was fun. The episode was called "Magic Locket" and when we were finished shooting, I kept half of the prop locket.

I did *The Capture of Grizzly Adams* [a 1982 TV movie] in Utah — we had a good shoot on that. For that show, they found me a marvelous pair of old, broken-

What, me retire?? June Lockhart's professional career began when she was a toddler in the early 1930s and has continued into the second decade of the 21st century.

in, wonderful boots, and they fit so well that the wardrobe mistress said, "You're gonna be doing more Westerns. Take these with you!" So far, *The Capture of Grizzly Adams* was one of my last Westerns. I'd love to do more. Well, *Lassie* might as well have been a Western, with all the outdoor scenes. Oh my God, out there (again) in Simi Valley from early morning 'til late nights. It absolutely could have been a Western; you could rewrite and shoot 'em again and have an Old West setting. Lassie's best friend could be a horse!

I look back on all the Westerns I did and I think, "Isn't it grand?" I thoroughly enjoyed them.

Fess Parker
AN IN-DEPTH Q&A

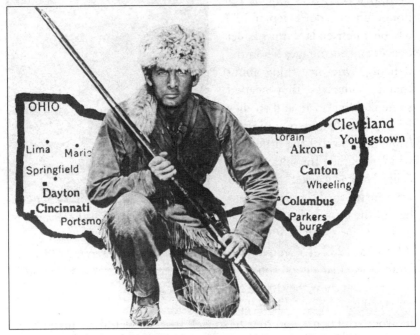

Back in 1951, Fess Parker gave himself 36 months to make it in show business or ax the idea. The role of Indian fighter Davy Crockett came at almost the last minute.

The son of a tax assessor, Fess Parker was a 6'5", 26-year-old Navy veteran when he went out to California in 1950 and studied at USC's School of Theater. He soon landed a role in a West Coast touring production of Mister Roberts *and then began his motion picture career with supporting parts. His comic role in the giant-ants movie* Them! *[1954] led directly to his historic casting in the star-making title role in the ABC-TV anthology series* Disneyland's *"Davy Crockett" trilogy.*

Also seen on TV as Daniel Boone *(in NBC's same-name '60s series), Parker blazed a trail of success in other fields as well: The courtly, silver-haired actor went from Hollywood to vines, running a winery and an inn and developing other real estate in the Los Olivos, California, area.*

Q: For the first time in my interviewing career, I'm going to begin with a one-word question: "Fess"?!

PARKER *[laughs]*: It's a surname. The gentleman who inspired my grandmother to name my father Fess was Dr. Simeon Fess, the president of Antioch College…later a United States Senator…a close friend of Will Rogers. Mentioned as a possible presidential candidate of 1932. His granddaughter Margaret Fess I met when she was a reporter for the *Detroit Free Press* — that tells you how long ago *that* was *[laughs]*. And then another of the Fesses was a judge in Indiana, I believe.

When my dad, who was born in 1900, got to his 20s, the cool thing in America was to have initials. He didn't like "Fess" because people always wanted to know where that came from, so he adopted the initial E. and became known as F.E. Parker. About the time I got to high school, I asked him, "What is my name?" "F.E. Parker, Jr." I asked, "Well…what is *your* name?" "*Fess* E. Parker." I said, "Well, there's an inconsistency here, Dad…!" *[laughs]* And I told him, "I'm gonna be Fess." Then I didn't have a name for E., so I looked up all the Es and I found that Fess *Elisha* Parker, Jr., was rather rhythmic. *My* son is named Fess Elisha Parker III, and then *he* has a son named Fess Clayton. So there's a *few* more years of "Fess" to be put up with…!

Q: The story of your landing the role of Davy Crockett begins with your appearance in a small part in the "giant ant" movie Them!

PARKER: *Them!* led to "Davy Crockett" because Jim Arness [one of the stars of *Them!*] was one of the people they were lookin' at to play Davy Crockett, and that's why Walt Disney ended up watching *Them!*

And I've always said to myself, "Walt probably asked, 'How much would Arness cost?' and then '*This* fellow [Parker] we ought to be able to get real economical!'" *[laughs]*

Q: Your first movie, in 1952, was a Universal Western called Untamed Frontier. *Had any TV parts preceded that?*

PARKER: No. *Untamed Frontier* was Joseph Cotten, Shelley Winters. Cotten didn't know Western boots and on location he threw his back out trying to get in or out of 'em *[laughs]*, so we went back to the studio and they put me in a picture with Tony Curtis and Piper Laurie [*No Room for the Groom*, 1952]. Finally when that was over, Cotten was ready to go ahead. So I did two pictures back to back. And then my next picture was with Gary Cooper, *Springfield Rifle* [1952]. The director Andre de Toth was very, very good to me, and I worked in a number of Westerns for him. Then I eventually got to *Them!* And after that, I was…not what they call "hot," but I was getting noticed. I was up for a role in *Gunsmoke*. While I was doing the "Crockett" thing, they started *Gunsmoke* and Jim Arness took that, and that was a marvelous career, 20 years.

Q: You were up for Gunsmoke's *Marshal Dillon, or a different part?*

PARKER: I never knew for sure, but they were going to interview me. Probably I was up for the Chester part, I guess.

Q: According to the old articles about you, at the beginning of your career you gave yourself 36 months to figure out if you could make a go of it in the picture business.

PARKER: That's true. In the summer of 1951 I was 26 and I thought, "I'll take three years and see what happens. If I can't do *this* [make it as an actor], I'll find something else." That period of 36 months began on Labor Day 1951, and I was hired by Walt Disney for "Davy Crockett" in August 1954.

Q: Right under the wire! Did you have other jobs at the same time you were making your earliest movies?

PARKER: In the first year, I moved refrigerators and stoves with a friend of mine, an actor named John Wiley. We made like a dollar an hour. I did inventories for department stores and…whatever I could do. It was typical actor's scramble.

When the 36 months began in September 1951, before *Untamed Frontier*, I had no agent. So I got the list of agents in Hollywood and I started with the A's, and no one would talk to me until I got to the Rs *[laughs]*. Wynn Rocamora was a successful agent who wasn't able to handle me,

Parker feels that playing a guitar and singing for Walt Disney in their initial meeting helped win him the Crockett role.

but he said one of his associates might. I was sent down the hall and I met a guy named Bill Barnes, a retired postal worker who had become a Hollywood agent. He asked me if I could find Warner Brothers and I said sure, so I went in there. [Casting director] Bill Tinsman asked me if I ever played baseball. I said yeah. He asked, "Hardball?" and I said, "Well, is there any other kind?" *[laughs]* Brynie Foy was a Warner Brothers producer, and when I walked in his office and he said, "My God, you look the part. Can you act?" I said, "Oh, yes *sir*!" They wanted to do a screen test and they gave me the script [for *The Winning Team*, 1952], but three days later they called me and said they *weren't* going to do the screen test, they were going to use an actor they had under contract. I said, "If you don't mind tellin' me, who are you going to use?" They said, "Ronald Reagan." I lost my first film opportunity to Ronald Reagan!

Incidentally, without those three years of playing little parts, and becoming a little more comfortable on sets, I would have been a disaster.

Disneyland's "Davy Crockett" trilogy wrote an amazing new chapter in TV history with mountaintop-high ratings and unprecedented merchandising.

Q: Did Walt Disney ever tell you what he saw in you, in the character you played in Them!, *that made him think of you as Davy Crockett?*

PARKER: No. I went out and I read for Crockett and I visited with Bill Walsh, the producer, and Tom Blackburn, who wrote the script. I saw them on two occasions, and on the third occasion Walt Disney came into the room and we left and we went down to a little room where we had a private interview, just the two of us in this little tiny writers' office. It didn't take him long to find out where I was from and how much I'd done — which was very little *[laughs]*! But he asked me, he said, "I see you brought your guitar." God knows why I did that, because I was not a musician. I was so poor a player of the guitar that I couldn't sing anybody else's song, I had to make up my own — I could only play something I'd made up myself. He said, "Why don't you play me something?," and I said, "Well, Mr. Disney, I wrote this…" and I sang him a little song I had written called "Lonely," about the sound of a train whistle. Well, what I didn't realize until just a few months ago — even though I did *The Great Locomotive Chase* [1956] for him — was that perhaps I ["connected" with him] at that moment, because that *was* a subject that he was passionate about — trains. He had trains in his backyard *[laughs]!* There's now a great book about Walt and his love of trains [*Walt Disney's Railroad Story*].

Q: So you were in talks for "Davy Crockett" for a while before you first met Disney?

PARKER: The interviews with the producer and writer were over a period of two and a half to three weeks, and when I came in the last time, they set up this thing with Walt. When they signed me, I was assigned to Walt himself. Not to the studio. And there were ramifications to that. When the movie *Bus Stop* [20th Century-Fox's 1956 filmization of the Broadway play] came along, I sensed that that was a movie I could do well in. It had not been cast at that point, and I wanted to throw my hat in the ring. Mr. Disney was the only boss I had, and I got a copy of the play and I brought it in to Walt and I said, "I'd love to play the cowboy in the movie." He read the play and then he sent me an interoffice memo, I still have it somewhere: "From Walt, To Fess, Don't think this is the kind of material you should do." Which I didn't — that was the end of that! I lost the opportunity to compete for that. Also, at one point when we were doing the *Locomotive Chase* picture, I was riding in a car in Georgia with Walt and Jeffrey Hunter, who was my co-star, on the way to a location. Jeffrey said that he'd had this great experience playing in *The Searchers* [1956] for John Ford, and Walt turned to me and he said, "They wanted *you* for that." *[Pause]* That ruined my trip.

Q: That was the first time you found out about it?

PARKER: Never knew about it. John Ford asked for me for *The Searchers.*

Q: So you have a million reasons to be grateful to Walt Disney but also a couple to be un*happy with the arrangement.*

PARKER: I understand perfectly and I have no animus over it. The Disney Studio was not, in those years, in that decade, really fixated on motion pictures. 'Cause even at the time I went to play Davy Crockett, Disneyland was incubating back there — they were actually working on it. There was no one in the organization who said, "Well, if you have a character that you have made recognizable around the world, there's value in that." So eventually I was being given the opportunity to play bit parts again. And I just said, "Well, I can't go backwards," and I had an amicable dissolution, and I walked away from five years of contract.

Q: Besides Arness, do you know if anyone else was up for the role of Davy Crockett?

PARKER: Bill Walsh once showed me a list of over 30 people. The business was *full* of action-type actors. It was just one of those miracles in show business that somehow they figured I could do it.

Q: Most of "Davy Crockett" was shot in Tennessee, correct?

PARKER: North Carolina at first, Cherokee, North Carolina. That little town is in the middle of the Cherokee Indian Reservation, so all of the Indians *were* Indians. Then we moved into Tennessee, we shot along the river in (I think) Johnson City and Chattanooga. And then into Nashville, where we did the Congressional [scenes] using the Tennessee State House. I was in shock there because the governor of the state was only two years older than I was. I got to know him well. His name was Frank G. Clement, he was a lawyer-turned-politician, a handsome guy with a beautiful family, lovely wife and two children. I was just shocked.

Q: Were the interiors shot in Hollywood?

PARKER: No, they were all shot on location except what you saw of interiors in the Alamo section. Those were shot on a stage at Disney.

Q: Did anybody have an inkling that this was going to be something special, or was it just three episodes of a kiddie show?

PARKER: I think that it was a total surprise. The record ["The Ballad of Davy Crockett "] was number one on the hit parade for four months, and nominated for an Academy Award. But it was knocked out of the competition because somebody said that, even though "Davy Crockett" ended *up* as a motion picture [the episodes were edited together into a feature-length theatrical release], it was a made-for-television movie and *not* a motion picture.

Q: When were you first alerted to the fact that the ratings were through the roof, that Davy Crockett was really catching on?

PARKER: I have a friend who's had a long, long career in motion pictures. Name's Morgan Woodward. After he got out of the Air Force, where he had been an officer, he lived in Arlington, Texas, and he was married, and so he was looking for a business. So he bought a Foster's Freeze franchise. It was a hamburger-and-milkshake kind of a place. He wasn't very happy with that. I finished with "Davy Crockett" in December 1954 and I went home to visit my parents, who were living in Fort Worth. Went over to see Morgan and we went off to lunch. The studio had asked me not to cut my hair because there'd maybe be some retakes or something.

Q: So you were still very recognizable as Davy Crockett.

PARKER: Right. So we went to some little hamburger joint down the road and sat, and the whole time we were having our hamburgers, there was an old lady behind the cash register and she kept looking at me. Finally we went up to pay the bill and she said, "Young man…have I seen you on television?" I said, "Well, maybe you *have*," because the first episode had been shown on the 15th. And she said, "Well, *I* knowed it! I watch wrasslin' every Saturday night!"

Q: [Laughs] You think she had *seen you in "Davy Crockett" but got mixed up?*

PARKER: I'm not exactly sure *where* that came from. But that was the first "mmmmaybe." Incidentally, Morgan Woodward had an acting background and a singing background and I thought he oughta come out to California. And he did, and I introduced him to the Disney Studio and he got started in *The Great Locomotive Chase*.

Q: You did a lot of traveling around the country as Davy Crockett.

PARKER: They had me in Houston and then quickly into Washington, D.C., and I met Sam Rayburn and Lyndon Johnson and all the

Congressmen from Tennessee and Texas. And then went to Philadelphia, and in Independence Hall by the Liberty Bell the National Rifle Association had a Congressional Medal of Honor Marine general present me with one of my most prized possessions today, a long rifle. It's well over 200 years old. It was a black tie event, a retirement dinner for the assistant Secretary of Defense, Anderson, and the dais was loaded with Senators and generals and admirals. I was sitting up on the dais in my costume —

Q: Your buckskins?

PARKER: Yes. And this is a black tie deal! The dais was 50 yards long, it was the biggest thing I'd ever seen. There were 30 or 40 people in a line, asking me to sign autographs — and there was a speaker trying to speak! So finally I said, "I'll be glad to stay…right now I just think we're [disrupting the event]." Then I'm sitting there, and the Senators and generals are sending me their programs, would I sign them for 'em *[laughs]*? After that I got up and presented a replica of my long rifle to Secretary Anderson.

Pretty soon [the Disney organization] had Buddy Ebsen and me into the studio and said, "You guys are gonna go out on the road and tour." I went to 42 cities in all, a lot of them by myself. We started in Texas and ended up at the Mastbaum Theater in Philadelphia. They let all the kids out of school in Detroit, and those streets were sort of like the Pope's audience — people as far as you could see. We couldn't leave for several hours.

Q: I can't even begin to guess at the number of celebrities who have complained that their lives are screwed up because "success came too fast." I can't think of a guy to whom success came faster so tell me — can that really screw up a person's life?

PARKER: Not really! Fortunately, I was 30 when the bulk of that descended on my shoulders. It *was* a strain. I went to those 42 cities, and then they sent me to Europe. And the European Disney organization felt, well, if they did 42 cities in America, *we* can do that and maybe a few *more!* All in all, I think I went to 13 countries on that tour. I ended up in Italy, and Walt sent me a message saying, "Take two weeks and do anything you want to do." I said, "I just want to come home!" I was worn out. A great experience, and so educational for me.

You might have the idea that being a successful actor is [the epitome of success], but in the places I went, I met families like the one that had a department store in Alabama. It was generational — there was an older man, a younger man and grandchildren [in charge], and I see this magnificent department store, and what a real success amounted to. I always remembered that family, and other businesspeople that I met. And I had

Parker embarked on a whirlwind publicity tour on behalf of "Davy Crockett," frequently accompanied by Buddy Ebsen who played Davy's sidekick George Russel.

good advice from a guy who was my business manager, when I got to a point where I could *have* one, and he said, "You knew, Fess, your lifestyle may be difficult to support when your career wanes. And it *will* wane." Even in Spain *[laughs]!* That caused me to focus on trying to figure out how to build some security, aside from what money they gave me.

Q: What can you recall about Jeff York, who played river pirate Mike Fink on "Davy Crockett"?

PARKER: Jeff was a great guy. 'Sorry I didn't see more of him in the intervening years. 'Had a plan to see him again and, before I could get up to where he was living in Santa Cruz, he had a stroke. I had briefly been on the board of trustees of the Motion Picture Country Hospital, in the '60s, and one of my friends, Billy Bakewell, a wonderful actor [also in "Davy Crockett," as Major Norton], was still on the board. So I got a-hold of Billy and I said, "You know, Jeff hasn't got the money to be treated, and he has no family that can take care of him." And so we got a-hold of Lucille Martin, who's still affiliated with Disney, and said, "Could you please ask someone, maybe Michael Eisner, if we can get Jeff in the Motion Picture Country Hospital?" The policy at the Motion Picture Country Hospital is, if you have a terminal condition, you're more likely to get in. But if you had a stroke and you're incapacitated and you're gonna live for who-knows-how-long, that was harder. But we did get Jeff in. I went out to see him there. Obviously, it's heart-wrenching to see somebody who's lost speech and mobility, and can only express themselves through one eye. Jeff was very, very strong, and he lingered *far* too long in that condition.

Q: "Role model" is a term that gets bandied around a lot these days — actors and sports stars and singers and any body who gets big enough, pretty soon certain people are bearing down on them, "You're popular now so you have to watch yourself, you have to be a role model." Do actors-sports stars-singers-Davy Crocketts have an obligation to —

PARKER *[interrupting]* : *Yes*. In *my* view. Your success comes off of the interest of the public. And if they have a conception of you that maybe you unwittingly presented, then I think that it's a good thing for you to remember that exclusively in your public life. Now, if you're somebody who has a proclivity which is not known, which is not exploited, I don't think you have any obligations to change your life as long as you're not breaking any laws. But there's a difference. So [having the responsibilities of a role model] has helped me, because I am just like everybody else, I'm a human being. Buddy Ebsen gave me the best advice. I think we were talking about some of the lovely-lady opportunities that present themselves *[laughs]*, and he said, "Just remember this: If you're gonna do somethin' like that, do it with somebody who has just as much to lose as you do."

Veteran tough guy Mike Mazurki tries to stomp a mudhole in Parker in one of "Davy Crockett"'s exciting donnybrooks.

Q: I dunno...if I was an actor and I played a role and suddenly I was being told I had to help instill values in the kids of America...I think my first reaction would be, "Wait a minute, I don't want that job, I'm just an actor!" But it never spooked you?

PARKER: No. As a matter of fact, I once considered being a teacher — that was sorta what I was thinking about becoming, if I couldn't make a living in films. Actually, I think the thing I'm proudest of, and had the least to do with, is the writing and the presentation of the [Crockett] character that the Disney team put out there. That gave me the *gift* of being able to represent a positive image.

I was gifted with the philosophy that a man's color, or his condition, didn't remove him from being a human being and being treated that way. That was inculcated in all of this material that they wrote into the character of Crockett. Being straightforward and truthful. Today I'm shocked and saddened by cadets at VMI and Air Force Academy and colleges and universities, making a game out of cheating themselves of their educational opportunities for…for…*[Pause]* I'm not *sure* what for! Today people have no respect for the government. Do *I* have it all the time? Definitely not! But I'm interested, and that's the difference. I've found that many people are not interested at all. That's the tragedy. We have a gift and we don't know it.

Q: Many people got rich off of Davy Crockett, what with all the merchandising and everything. What did you get out of it money-wise apart from your actor's salary?

PARKER: Well, I never have pushed this, but I'll be candid with you. Walt Disney gave me ten percent of the Walt Disney-Davy Crockett merchandise. Then when I changed agents and engaged the legendary Ray Stark, he went into the studio and negotiated five or six times what I was being paid. Walt didn't want to pay that, so he gave my contract over to the studio. And I think they took that moment and took away my merchandise rights in lieu of about $5000 more a week.

Q: You think you got that raise instead *of the ten percent.*

PARKER: When I asked for a raise, I think as part of the trade for giving me quite a bit more money a week than I was getting, I think that [ten percent] was dealt away from me. And so I never really made what was certainly indicated was possible. But I'll tell you one thing about it: It *was* true, that I was promised that [percentage], and that was publicized. So I decided — this was probably my best acting job ever — I decided that I would act as if that money existed somewhere. I didn't live lavishly or anything, but I lived well…I lived in Bel-Air, I lived at Hope Ranch. And I had an opportunity, through this [image], that I could call the vice-president of a company, or the president, or somebody that I need to talk to; introduce myself; and normally, if it was possible, I would eventually get an audience.

Parker went from a dollar-an-hour furniture mover and inventory counter for department stores to TV immortality as pioneer hero Crockett and, later, TV's Daniel Boone *(pictured).*

Q: We hear actors complaining all the time that they got typecast. As some-body who very rarely was seen out of buckskins, is it a curse or a blessing or somewhere in between?

PARKER: In the long term, a blessing. How many wonderful actors there were who, unless you are a real film buff, are not remembered. I've had a career of enforcement, *re*inforcement, and it has lasted close to 50 years.

Q: Does everything you touch turn to gold? You're plucked from obscurity and become the biggest thing on TV, you come up here and look at all this *[the inn, winery, etc.]. what have you tried to do that didn't work out?*

PARKER: Oh, I turned my back on one or two major things. I am responsible for opening up the Silicon Valley. I had a large property there, and sold it to Marriott. I shouldn't have, but I did. And there've been other opportunities. But I've been lucky…

Q: In 1988 you wrote a "Davy Crockett" sequel in which Davy hadn't died at the Alamo. Without giving away the store, what would have happened to him in your story?

PARKER: I had a wonderful idea and I could not understand the lack of interest by Disney. I went in to [Jeffrey] Katzenberg and I said, "Buddy Ebsen and I are both getting older, but we still can *do* something. And Buddy is *up* to this. I have a story, and that *is*…," and I told him the story. Gen. Santa Ana was very astute and he recognized that there was some hostage value to Crockett and his friend Georgie. As badly wounded as they might have been, they were taken to an obscure prison outside of Mexico City. Years passed, the fortunes of Gen. Santa Ana waned, and now Buddy was a trustee in the prison and Davy still had leg irons. The time had gone by and they looked like *we* now look [in 1988]. One day they have a furtive conversation, "We better get out of here and we're gonna *die* in here." There was a Katy Jurado-kind of lady in the kitchen, and she thought that Georgie was real cute and she was always after him — much to his annoyance! So they cooked up a deal where Georgie played up to her and he got some grease and a saw and a file and they got ready to escape. They managed to get into a wagon that was gonna take something *out* of the prison, and then they took over the wagon. Cesar Romero was still around, and he was gonna be the commandant.

Q: You hoped, or you asked him?

PARKER: Well, he was "the visual" that I used for the telling of the story. The commandant was furious about the escape, and the Mexican dragoons were after us. Finally the wagon fell apart but we did make it into the woods, had various different adventures. We got down to where

Crockett (Parker) and Major Tobias Norton (William Bakewell) were enemies on-screen, but Parker liked Bakewell enough to write a role for him in a proposed 1980s Crockett sequel. It never came to pass. Parker died in 2010.

Cancun is now, only there was no Cancun, there was just a little village. We were looking to find a way to get back [to the U.S.], and a ship came in and anchored to take on water and broke out an American flag. We got somebody to row us out there and asked, "Could we work our way back to the States?" The captain was sort of a roguish-looking guy and he said, "Sure. Glad to have you." Well, they got the water and they started out, and Georgie was sicker than the Devil — he couldn't even be on deck. Finally he was feelin' better and he came up one night when Davy was lookin' up at the stars. "Georgie," Davy said, "by lookin' at these stars I can tell we're goin' the wrong way." Fade out, fade up, another anchorage, they were off the shore of West Africa, takin' on slaves.

The slave ship was goin' through the Caribbean, Georgie and Davy was doin' everything they could for the guys chained down in the hold. There was a splendid-looking black man, the nominal leader of the group down there, and they were planning some sort of revolt. Davy and Georgie found out about it and they said, "Why don't you do *this* instead? Trust us, we've been in your position. We don't want to slaughter the crew or the captain, we want to put them off — give 'em a chance." So they took the boat, they put the captain off, and they sailed up near the mouth of the Mississippi. They got off the boat, and this black gentleman, said, "I've heard about America and I'd like to go with you. My friends can sail the boat back." Fine. So the three of them went to New Orleans; Davy went one direction to get something and Georgie and the black man was doin' somethin' else when some Southerners came out of a saloon and saw the black man and one said, "Doesn't that look like the boy that left the Miller plantation last week?," "Why, it sho' does"!" So they came over and they tried to take him, and he and Georgie put up a fight. Then I came along. And *this* was my favorite scene: Billy Bakewell was in a phaeton with the big hat and the ladies with the parasols, and the phaeton passed this minor riot goin' on, and he did one of those double-takes, like, "Naw. It *couldn't* be!" *[laughs]*

Anyway, we finally got out of that pickle and we sat down and said, "Well, where do you want to go?" And Davy and Georgie agreed that we'd like to go back to the Alamo one more time. We made our way back there and arrived on March 6 [the anniversary of the fall of the Alamo]...all the townspeople were out and the politicians and there were speeches, and they were reading off the names of the defenders. Davy and Georgie looked at each other and *[Parker grimaces, shrugs]*. "We're not cut out to be heroes. Let's get out of here!" *[laughs]* And off over the hill. And that was the end of it.

I thought that that would be an interesting movie, and that Disney would welcome it. *Now*, today [2004], they're doing *The Alamo* and I just hope that they really have great success with it because the Texas story is not just the Alamo, good guys-bad guys. It's a much broader canvas. And in a way it represents a lot of what's going on in our country today, about the war [against terrorism]. A lot of people didn't want to fight Mexico — they had interests.

Q: Years and, I hope, more years from now, you and DC meet on that big mountaintop in the sky. Who's going to speak first, and what's he going to say?

PARKER: Well, given his reputation — I'm gonna be quiet *[laughs]*.

Bill Phipps
RIDES WITH
THE *CAVALRY COMMAND*

William Phipps as he appeared in a Grade-A Western, 1955's The
Violent Men *with Glenn Ford, Barbara Stanwyck and Edward G.
Robinson.*

In 1947, the same year that Bill Phipps made his movie debut in RKO's Crossfire, *he first hit the Western trail, appearing as a lawman in that studio's* The Arizona Ranger. *The Tim Holt-Jack Holt-starring B Western was the first of scores of sagebrush roles, big- and small-screen, for the Indiana-born actor. For his most interesting Western experience, however, he left the sound-stages of Hollywood far behind, traveling to the Philippines in 1957 to co-star in a cavalry drama based on historical incidents that had taken place in those very islands.*

BILL PHIPPS: *Cavalry Command* is set in the year 1902 when the U.S. took possession of the Philippines from the Spanish. When it was offered to me, I jumped at the idea. In 1957 I was only 35 years old, and I thought it would be a big adventure. Plus which, when I was in the Navy in World War II, one of my many, many stops was in the Philippines; we were carrying cargo for the Marines and the soldiers who had made beachheads there. We were anchored off the island of Mindanao, and I had a wisdom tooth removed on shore, on a little tiny island called Guiuan. I didn't get to see much of the Philippines at that time, and I would have liked to.

Cavalry Command was the first Filipino movie ever made with American stars [John Agar, Phipps, Richard Arlen, Myron Healey] and with all-Filipino money. We shot on the island of Luzon; on the northern tip there's a village called Vigan. I'm "the love interest" in the picture: In the beginning, my character is sick, malaria or something, and I fall off my horse, and I'm nursed back to health by a Filipina young lady played by Cielito Legaspi, who I think was only 16 years old. In one scene, as she's giving me a sponge bath, we were supposed to kiss. Well, the interesting thing about the Filipinos is that they have this "morality." The culture of those people is very different from ours, and her relatives and her boy-friend wouldn't let her do the kiss. And Cielito herself, who as I say was like 16, was very closed-in, very timid, very shy. One-word conversations: "How are you?"—"Fine," "Good morning"—"Good morning," and that would be the end of it. Finally [writer-director] Eddie Romero talked her into it, and she agreed provided everybody who was not needed left the set. What happened, too, was that they "cheated" on the camera angle as I grabbed her and pulled her towards me, and we kinda faked it. And then she ran off the set crying, *sobbing.* This was a big deal in the Philippines; in Manila, it was front page news in all the papers! The newspaper story described how she ran from the set crying, and featured our picture, with our faces close to each other. And it was *shocking* news!

As you probably know, John Agar was an alcoholic. I mean, a *raaaging* alcoholic. To get the picture finished, I had to baby-sit him, because a couple of times they had to stop shooting, and shoot stuff over, because he was too drunk, or he was still recovering and his eyes were obviously glazed over. So I would sit with him in his hotel room night after night, drinking Cokes and coffee and watching TV, and keeping him engaged

in conversation, just to keep him sober and out of trouble. I had my own hotel suite, it had all the accommodations you can imagine, and John had *his* own, but to keep him sober, I used to go to his room and sit up with him all night long. We never talked about the fact that I was there to keep him sober, but it was tacit. Nobody asked me to do that, I just sort of gravitated to it. John and I liked each other, we got along well together, and so I went around to his room and it just sort of *happened*. You have to be delicate and finesse those things; otherwise people might rebel. If someone were to say to him, "I'm comin' over to your room and sittin' with you and watchin' TV to keep you from drinkin'," it probably *wouldn't* happen, he would resent it. I would, you would too, if it was put to you that way. So…it just sorta *happened*. If I hadn't done that, we wouldn't have been able to finish the picture.

I didn't like Richard Arlen at all. He was moronic. He drank; and he was a problem; and he almost got himself killed because he insulted the

Filipinos. He was either hung over or half-drunk and, talking about the crew at the top of his voice, he called them sons of bitches. And they heard him — it was awful! You have to be *very*, very delicate with people like that, in their own country. He didn't know it, he was unaware of it, but he almost got killed. I was aware of it because I was real tight with the Filipinos; I loved them, they loved me. And Myron Healey almost

Bill Phipps' acting résumé has been peppered with Westerns almost from Day One, as can be seen from these autographed Desperadoes of Dodge City *(1948) and* Jesse James vs. the Daltons *(1954) lobby cards.*

got killed, too, and he didn't realize it, 'cause he was using profanity in front of the Filipinos when their wives and girlfriends and daughters were around. You can *do* that in Hollywood, but not there. Arlen and Healey would get drunk and they'd start swearing, and they never even realized the extent and the magnitude of their effrontery — or that Eddie Romero saved their lives. John Agar, on the other hand, was a lovable guy and he never ever offended anybody, he was never overbearing with people. It was amazing: He was the worst abuser of the booze but he never got belligerent, he never got cross, he never insulted anybody.

Cockfighting is as much of the Filipinos' heritage as bullfighting is with the Spaniards. I went to a bullfight, and there was a female bullfighter with blonde hair from the United States, and she was *awful*. Agar and I were in the stands together, and he was drunk, and he was *booing* her at the top of his lungs: "Booooo! *Booooo!*" John got everybody *else* to booing too. It must have been very embarrassing for her, but she *was* terrible. Then, later on, he ran down and got into the fucking bullring *[laughs]* — can you believe that? They had to get him out of there before he got killed!

The exteriors were shot in Vigan, a village on the northern tip of the island, and the interiors in Manila. We were making the trip from Vigan to Manila by automobile, it's 200 miles or more, so we made a stop at a place called Baguio, a resort area where all of the richest people, the Marcoses and everybody, go because it's high elevation. In the Philippines, there's terrible, oppressive heat…very unpleasant…and mosquitoes. Really bad. As a place to live, in a word, it sucks *[laughs]*. But in Baguio, it's very cool, just a beautiful spot. So coming back, our convoy stopped there, and Agar and I were in the bar having a drink. Well, there's *always* somebody who has to challenge a celebrity, *always*. Some smartass came up to us and started getting very insulting, insinuating that John was not really John Agar. Agar pulled out his wallet and slammed it on the bar, to try to prove it by showing the guy some i.d., and just then the guy got *too* belligerent, and a couple of MP-type fellows intervened and got us out of there before it got really bad. The next day in makeup, John and I were talking about it, and John said, "Little does he know, but I'm *really* Shirley Temple!" *[laughs]* That's funny, isn't it?, that he could poke fun at himself like that? That cracked me up, I laughed about that all day. So you can see how funny *he* was!

Oh, speaking about Manila, the director Eddie Romero one day said, "Manila is far worse than the wild west *ever* was" — and he was so right. I remember, when we were in Vigan, one morning I got up and I was told that somebody was killed during the night. And everybody was very nonchalant about it! I said, "What *happened?*" and I was told, "Somebody cut his head off with a machete." There was not much said about it, nobody cared, nobody talked about, it wasn't big news. It was just like…"Well… things *happen*." Romero, by the way, was beautiful, just a great guy. He was a writer-producer-director, and because his father was a Filipino ambassador to England, Eddie spoke perfect English.

In Manila, the hotel where John and I stayed was the Filipinas, sort of new at the time. The mayor of Manila, Lacson, was a swashbuckler-type, like the Filipinos could be, and every day at lunch hour, he would be there with his bodyguards. One time Agar was in the hotel bar drinking and having fun, and Lacson somehow took offense to it, and one of the guards put a .45 automatic to Agar's head! Of course he didn't shoot Agar — obviously *[laughs]* — but still, that's a horrible thing to do. I wasn't there at the time but I was told about it later. Somehow or other, it "cooled off," and that was the end of it. But that's how it is in Manila, as I told you before about Eddie Romero saying it was worse than the wild west.

[Actor] Pancho Magalona was also in it. Because he was a matinee idol in the Philippines, he said to me that he was going to come to Hollywood and get into movies here. I tried to be as delicate as possible, I tried to say, "Y'know, Pancho…it wouldn't *work*. You're big here but you couldn't *make* it in Hollywood." He didn't like hearing that, and he got a little miffed at me. Even trying to be delicate and diplomatic, I punctured his ego by advising him not to try it. But what I was saying was true: The American public's not in love with Filipinos to begin with; and what's handsome to

According to A-one researcher Robert Kiss, Cavalry Command *"truly seems to have been a picture about which no U.S. distributor gave a damn. It opened simultaneously at three California theaters on November 6, 1963, and those three prints seem to have then traveled the nation gaining very few bookings as a second-feature through to September 1964 — at which point the movie turned up on television!" Right:* Cavalry Command *was called by its original title,* The Day of the Trumpet, *in this 1958 Filipino trade ad.*

them [to Filipinos] is not handsome to *us*. Then Pancho *did* come here to Hollywood, not so many years later, and he did one movie at MGM [1963's *The Hook* with Kirk Douglas], and I never heard of him again. You see my point, don't you? How could he rise to "matinee idol" status with American audiences? It just wouldn't *happen*. What I *wanted* to say to him was, "You haven't got a fuckin' chance, Pancho!" *[laughs]* "Don't be stupid! You're making millions of pesos *here*, you've got movie audiences at your *feet*. Don't *blow* it!" But how can you say that to somebody? Hard to do, right? He was an example of somebody who is a hero in his home country, letting it go to his head. You can go to any country in the world and you could find an idol, the top *this* or the top *that* — but nobody cares anywhere *else*.

When the picture was finished, they kept me for an extra week, and instead of taking pay for it, I asked 'em to get me an airline ticket for a trip around the world. And so instead of coming back home across the Pacific, I went around the world and stopped in a lot of countries, flying on 13 different airlines just for the kicks. The following year, Eddie Romero came to Hollywood because he was about to make a movie in the Philippines called *Man on the Run*. I read the script and agreed to do it. He also needed somebody to play the part of a man who owns a jai alai court, a man whose son I kidnap for ransom. At one point we thought of Bob Lowery doing it, he was a good friend of mine; and we thought of some other people. Burgess Meredith and I were palling around at the time; we'd made the movie *The Man on the Eiffel Tower* [1950] in Paris together. Burgess and I were at Romanoffs, the very famous restaurant, and I said, "How would you like to go to the Philippines and make a movie, stay there about a month?" To make a long story short, he finally said, "Sure, I've got nothing to do right now, let's *do* it." So we did it.

To finish up on *Cavalry Command*, its original title [and its release title in the Philippines] was *The Day of the Trumpet*. When it was released in the U.S. in 1963 the title was changed to *Cavalry Command*, to make it sound more like a Western. As a movie, it's so-so, but I *loved* the experience of making it. The local people were wonderful, very hospitable. They treated me royally, and it was just great. If you make the effort to understand those people and see their way of life and their culture, it's very simple to get along with them. I loved making both movies there, and I'll tell you why: There is no pressure, nobody's in a hurry, there's no ado about the time or the schedule, they don't talk about budget. It's just, "Do it *your* way," "Take all the time you *want*." When you've got the feeling that you've got all the time in the world, can you imagine how relaxed you get when that happens? What a beautiful, beautiful way to make movies; it isn't done that way often enough. Most of my life, it's been "Hurry up," "We gotta hurry!," everybody's looking at their watch, "We have to do such-and-such," "No, we haven't got time!," "We're over-budget," blah blah blah blah blah blah blah. On *Cavalry Command* and *Man on the Run, none* of that. It was a "dream way" of making movies.

And I'll tell you [the "dream way" of being an actor], as far as I was concerned: When I was at the height of my working and acting ability and very "gung ho," I would spend all my time studying and working in Charles Laughton's acting group and going to see old films and reading up on art and on acting and on theater. I hated being distracted by, say, having to take care of my car, take care of my laundry, having to deposit checks and pay bills and so on. I would rather not have *seen* a check, I would rather not have *had* any money, because (like many actors) I didn't get into acting for the money, I got into it for the love of theater, for the

A long acting career, the respect of his peers; Phipps says, "What more could you ask for?"

love of acting, for the love of audiences. It's a compulsion: If you have talent as an actor, you are *compelled* to act, you have to find a way to do it. All of that other business having to do with money and bills and the mundane things — it gets in the way. This is a purist's way of thinking, I know, but I would love to have been able to spend all of my time and all of my efforts on the craft, the art of acting, instead of having to take care of those details. If somebody else could have taken care of all that other stuff and I would never have to see a bill, never have to have any money in my pocket, never have to spend anything — that would have been ideal. Then I could just *act.*

Paul Picerni
SCALPHUNTER!

Paul Picerni as the villainous Frank in The Scalphunters.
Variety described the hard-to-describe Western as "a satirical, slapstick, intellectual oater drama, laced with civil rights overtones, and loaded with recurring action scenes."

The 1968 Western The Scalphunters *came at a crossroads in the life and career of Paul Picerni: Worn down by the grind of starring in the TV soap opera* The Young Marrieds, *he developed diabetes and worried that he could no longer pursue acting as a livelihood. With some trepidation, he accepted a supporting role in* The Scalphunters *and waited to see if he was still up to the challenge of outdoor action movie-making...*

PAUL PICERNI: After *The Young Marrieds* was cancelled, I was out of work and physically exhausted. The stress of learning all those lines day in and day out for two years had taken its toll. I went to see my physician, Dr. Saliba, who gave me a complete physical and then sent me to the Sansum Clinic in Santa Barbara for two weeks of tests. It was determined that I had diabetes.

For the first time in my life, I felt defeated and really "down." I had never been sick before, so I didn't understand what was happening. From now on, I would have to watch what I ate. I couldn't drink wine or alcohol. I had to exercise regularly. I had to avoid sugar. I couldn't have a *donut*. I might black out from *low* blood sugar. I might go into a coma from *high* blood sugar. I was a mess. "My life is over. My career is ended." I thought I could never act again. That was my mental state.

With all of that, I was also out of work, and I had eight kids to support, all of them still in private schools. [Actor] Nick Cravat and I were very close friends; he was Uncle Nick to my kids. Nick and I would run at Crespi High School track in the morning several days a week, and when Burt Lancaster wasn't busy, he would run *with* us. At this time, Burt was preparing to make *The Scalphunters*, a fairly low-budget Levy-Gardner-Laven Western for United Artists release. Burt told me I could play one of the Scalphunters; it wasn't going to be much of a part, but the job would run for six weeks in Durango, Mexico.

Could I do it? Would I be able to go on location with my condition and perform? These were the thoughts that went through my head. Dr. Saliba assured me I would be physically capable of doing *The Scalphunt-ers*; I just had to take Diabanese pills before each meal and watch what I ate. I wasn't so sure. I knew *one* thing, though: I wouldn't have to worry about exercise. I'd be getting plenty of *that* riding horses and scalping Indians in the film!

In *The Scalphunters*, Burt Lancaster starred as a trapper who teams with an escaped slave (Ossie Davis) to recover his annual yield of furs, stolen by Telly Savalas' ruthless Scalphunter gang. Shelley Winters played Telly's cigar-smoking mistress and I was one of Telly's Scalphunters, along with

Dabney Coleman, Dan Vadis, several stuntmen and, of course, Nick Cravat. (Nick got his screen name "Cravat" from an old Western he had seen, an Oscar winner called *Cimarron* [1931] with Richard Dix as "Yancey Cravat." In fact, Nick's character name in *The Scalphunters* was Yancy!) The director was Sydney Pollack and *Scalphunters* was one of his first pictures; Burt had "discovered" him when Sydney was a dialogue director.

With a large family (eight kids!) to support, Paul Picerni worried when he was diagnosed with diabetes in the mid-1960s.

Nick and I flew down together to Mazatlán, taking two crates of equipment (pistols and rifles) with us. We were picked up at the airport by a studio driver and taken to Durango, where we met up with Telly. Durango was a small, sleepy town with a large Mexican federal prison. Nick and I and the rest of the "lowbrow actors" had rooms at a motel (right next door to the prison!), Telly had a suite at the Posada Duran and Burt Lancaster and Jackie Bone, the hairdresser with whom he was living, had a rented house. I knew I'd be getting my required exercise just by doing the action scenes in the movie, but I was happy to also learn that there was a nine-hole golf course where I could play on my days off.

I had heard that, early in Shelley Winters' career, around the time of *A Double Life* [1947], she and Burt had a romance. But now this was 20 years later and Shelley was quite matronly, a little overweight — not nearly as gorgeous as she was when she was young. Nevertheless, the first thing she did was make a move on Burt. But Burt didn't pay any attention. Then she made a move on Telly, who was playing her lover in the movie but had no intention of doing so in real life! Then she made a move on *me*, and I didn't take the bait. Finally she ended up with another one of the Scalphunters, Dan Vadis, an actor who had done muscleman and gladiator-type movies in Europe. After just a short time, Shelley and Dan were going at it pretty good.

One night we were getting ready to shoot a big outdoor scene featuring all the Scalphunters and six or eight girls playing Mexican hookers. The shot was to start on a goat on a spit over an open fire, and Dan was going to slice a piece of meat off the goat and sample it. Then the camera, on a big crane, would pull back and show the whole scene of the Scalphunters and all the women having a great time singing, dancing and making merry. As we were getting ready to rehearse, the prop man said to Dan, "Don't slice the meat off the goat in the rehearsals, or by the time we get to the take the goat will look lousy. Wait for the take." And Dan's reaction was to tell the prop man, "Ahhh, fuck you!" (Dan was always smoking pot or doing some kind of drugs, so he was always half out of it.) This was a big shot that we were preparing to do and a lot of rehearsal was required, and Dan kept slicing meat off the goat. Finally the prop man got a-hold of Sydney Pollack on the side and said, "Would you tell Mr. Vadis not to cut the goat in the rehearsals? Tell him to wait for the take. Otherwise, half the goat'll be gone!" So Sydney, up on the camera boom with the camera operator, politely called out, "Oh, Dan, Dan! Don't cut the meat in the rehearsal, wait for the take." And Dan said, "Fuck you!" — this time to Sydney Pollack the director!

Sydney said, "*What?*" and again Dan said, in front of the whole company, "Go *fuck* yourself!" And at that point, Sydney said, "Get off the set. You're fired!" Then Sydney said to the first assistant, "Send him home. Get him *out* of here." As Dan left, Sydney told me that I would be taking Dan's place in the shot, cutting the sliver of meat off the goat.

We were shooting close to a river and Dan wandered away, down toward its banks. Shelley went down there after him and they chatted and then she came back up to the set and went into a tirade: "You can't do that! You can't fire Dan! If you fire *him*, you fire *me* too!" — she screamed and yelled at Sydney for firing Dan. But Sydney was serious, and he had no intention of bringing Dan back. At that point, Burt stepped in and tried to pacify Shelley. Burt was one of the producers of the picture along with Levy, Gardner and Laven, and he knew they needed Shelley. He didn't give a shit about Dan, he could get another Scalphunter, but Shelley he needed! Shelley continued to make a scene, there was crying and sobbing, and eventually Burt said, "You make Dan come back here and apologize to Sydney in front of the whole company, and we'll take him back." And Dan, half-stoned, wouldn't do it! It must have been an hour before they got the situation resolved. Dan finally agreed to apologize, and we got on with the shot.

The day after Shelley put her job on the line by fighting for her lover, she returned to Hollywood because she was up for a Golden Globe for her performance in *Alfie* [1966] with Michael Caine. With the producers' blessings she attended the awards banquet (she didn't win) and came back two days later. In the meantime, Dan Vadis took up with one of the Mexican hookers and forgot all about Shelley! That was Dan for you! When Shelley came back and found out about this, she was ready to kill him right in front of everybody! They had a big fight and she called him a son of a bitch. And then *she* took up with Armando Silvestre, the Mexican actor who played the Indian chief in the show. That was Shelley for you!

Shelley would always be sweet as pie until she was well-established in a film, and then she would become a pain in the ass and very demanding. One day when we were sitting on the set, one of the producers, Jules Levy, came by. Spotting him, Shelley started to cry. With tears running down her cheeks, she said, "I don't understand it, Jules. Burt has his own makeup man, why don't I have *my* own makeup man? Why can't I get Bill Phillips down here? *You* know he's my makeup man, I want my own makeup man!"

"Shelley, we can't *afford* it," Jules said. "We've got two makeup men down here already, and we can't afford a third."

"Well, I want my own makeup man," Shelley insisted, continuing to cry. Jules finally said, "All right, all right, I'll fly Bill Phillips down. He'll be here tomorrow," and he walked away. As soon as he was out of earshot, the "tearful" Shelley instantly became the laughing Shelley and said, "Boy, I got him, didn't I, fellas? Pretty good performance, right?"

Once she did 35 takes in a scene with Telly. Telly had to take a frying pan out of the fire, walk a few steps, throw away whatever was in the pan and then walk back to the fire. She inevitably would get to a certain point in the scene and then say, "Oh, I would like to do it again." If it had been me in the scene with her, I would have wanted to punch her. But Telly went on and on and did it 35 times and had tremendous patience.

The thing that made this trip to Mexico so sensational for me was being with Telly. We'd worked together before [on the TV series] *The Untouchables*, but it was in Durango on *The Scalphunters* that we bonded and became such good friends that we saw each other constantly, day in and day out on the set, at dinner and at night. Something about Telly just registered with me. He was from New York and I'm from New York, but it was more than that, there was something about him. He was so bright and so clever. He was also a con man, but lovable and entertaining. And such a marvelous storyteller. Over the years, stories of his that I heard for the first time in Durango I heard 30 *more* times, as he'd relate them to other people, but he told them so well that I enjoyed them every time.

Durango was about 200 miles due east of the beautiful beach city of Mazatlán. In 1967, the Mazatlán Hotel was the best of the few hotels on the sandy beaches of Olas Altas Bay. One weekend we drove there in Telly's big Lincoln Town Car — me, Telly, Nick Cravat and Telly's go-fer, David Gross. We had a terrific time; there's great jumbo shrimp in Mazatlán! On Monday morning we headed back to Durango, where we had to be at work at ten o'clock.

When we got to the top of the mountain that separates Mazatlán from Durango, we ran out of gas. Telly always seemed to tempt fate: We started down the mountain with a dead engine, coasting, no power steering and no power brakes. Whenever I got into a dangerous situation with Telly driving, he would say either, "Don't worry, you're in your mother's arms!" or "I'm one of the top three drivers in the world." It was really precarious going down the mountain. Screeching around corners, the big Lincoln was straining to stay on the road. I did something I did numerous times when driving with Telly: I made an act of contrition and put my future in the hands of the Lord!

At last we reached the bottom of the mountain and rolled to a stop. In the middle of nowhere. It was about 9:15. No way would we get to work on time.

But with Telly's luck, the first vehicle that came along was a tow truck. It must have been Telly's guardian angel driving it! The driver sold us a can of gas and we were on our way. We got to work with ten minutes to spare!

Telly was making $5000 a week on *The Scalphunters* and getting $1500 a week per diem. But you'd think he was making a million. It was impossible to pick up a check when Telly was around. One night the Jaffe brothers [United Artists honchos] and Levy, Gardner and Laven, the producers, came down to Durango and we all went out to dinner — Burt, Shelley, Ossie Davis, Telly, Nick, me, Sydney Pollack — 14 of us. When the check came, *Telly* picked it up. I couldn't figure him out. With all that brass there, someone else should have taken it; Telly wasn't that big at the time. But I later learned from Telly that Omar Sharif had told *him*, "When you throw bread out to the ocean, it breaks up into small pieces and comes back to you on each wave a thousand fold." It's true. The more Telly spent, the more he made. I learned to do that too; I *love* to pick up checks. I'm old enough now to know that you can't take it with you. I've seen friends of mine die and leave millions, and then watched their children fight over it. So don't be afraid to pick up a check. The money will come back to you double and then some.

While on that *Scalphunters* location, I taught Telly how to play bridge because I knew that Burt liked bridge. Then, in order to have a fourth for bridge, Burt flew down Solly Biano, the Warner Brothers talent guy who had discovered Burt at the Pantages Theater and discovered *me* at the Las Palmas Theater. Every night the four of us would sit on the Posada Duran patio and play bridge. We'd be out there 'til three or four in the morning, and if we didn't have to work the next day we'd be at it 'til five or six, when the sun came up. We'd play for pesos, and every night Telly and I would owe them a bundle of pesos! Solly was an excellent player and so was Burt, and they were always partners; Telly and I were outclassed. But Burt loved beating us, he didn't give a damn. Every night Telly and I would owe Burt and Solly three, four hundred pesos, which didn't amount to a *lot* of money — one peso was about a dime.

This one night when we were playing, it must be two o'clock in the morning and Telly was sitting across from me, dozing; Burt was on my left; Solly on my right. Burt got a terrific hand and he bid "two no trump," which means that he had like 22, 24 points in his hand. (There's only 40 points in the whole deck.) When your partner bids two of anything, that's what's called a demand bid and you can't pass, you *must* name some suit. So Solly gave him a bid because he *had* to. Burt was tingling with excitement. But after it went around a few more times, I was able to tell that things weren't going well for Burt and Solly. I had 14 points in my hand, so when Burt got up to a slam bid, I said, "Double," which means whatever points we got in this hand would be doubled. With 14 points

Picerni at the Audie Murphy Museum in Greenville, Texas, in June 2010. He holds his autobiography Steps to Stardom, *in which he tells the story of his career, from his days as a Warner Brothers contract player to TV's* The Untouchables *and right up to into the 2000s.*

in my hand, I knew he *couldn't* make a slam bid. Burt looked at me and defiantly he said, "*Re*-double!" Well, when Solly put down the dummy and he didn't have a single point, Burt almost shit. He slammed the table hard enough that Telly came out of his doze, and then Burt and Solly started going back and forth at each other: "Solly, why the hell did you bid?," "Well, you gave me a demand bid!," "You shouldn't have bid with a hand like that!," "You gave me a demand bid, I *had* to bid!" Loud and excited, they started having a big argument — I was just barely holding in my laughter! Telly was now wide awake from all the yelling.

Finally they finished arguing, but Burt was still furious now, and also determined to play the hand out. To make a long story short, not only did we set them, but we set them six down, doubled and re-doubled, and it amounted to about 3000 points at a peso a point! I slapped the table and exuberantly I yelled out, "We *got* 'em, Telly, we *got* 'em! Finally, we beat the bastards!" I reached out across the table to shake Telly's hand — and Burt, furious, slapped me in the face!

"You're a *loser*," he growled at me. "You're a *born loser*. You been a loser all your fucking *life*!"

I grabbed his hand and through gritted teeth I said, "Don't you *do* that, Burt! What the hell's the matter with you? Are you fuckin' *crazy*?"

Telly looked at me and he started shaking his head like "no, no, no," trying to get across to me, "Don't go any further. Don't challenge him." But I was ready to challenge him — I didn't give a shit about Burt Lancaster or the movie or anything, because he had slapped me. It didn't really hurt, it was just two fingers across the cheek, but the mere fact that he slapped me made me furious. But I took Telly's unspoken advice "Don't take it any further." I threw his hand down, I stared at him, I got up from the table and I walked out.

I later went up to Telly's room and we talked about what had happened, rehashed it all, before I went to my motel and went to bed. The next day was Sunday and at about 10 or 11 o'clock Telly called me and said, "Listen, Burt just called me. He asked if I wanted to play golf today. I said, yeah, I'd love to. And then Burt said, 'Oh, bring Paul along too.'"

Inviting me to golf, that was Burt's way of apologizing. And I accepted the invitation (and Burt's unspoken apology) and I played golf with them. It was Telly and me against Burt and Jackie, his girlfriend. And inevitably they beat us at golf too!

An aside: Burt once said to me, "Why don't you get a group of your friends and we'll have a bridge game at your house?" My wife Marie invited about ten of our bridge friends over, along with Burt and his girlfriend Jackie Bone. We set up four four-player tables in the living room and had a big spread of cold cuts, drinks and other goodies on the dining room table. The evening was going great, Burt was having a good time, and all the other people were enjoying being in the same room playing bridge with the great Burt Lancaster. Suddenly all the "good vibes" stopped with a thundering roar: I was at a table with Burt and Marie and a delightful lady — I emphasize *lady* — named Mrs. Wainwright, Burt's partner, when in the process of bidding four spades, Burt let out with a resounding fart. Everybody at the four tables looked up and all talk ended. They all looked in our direction, astounded. Burt continued as if nothing had happened; "Your bid, Paul," he said quietly. I was dumbstruck.

He was so concentrated on his bridge hand that I don't think he knew what he did! Either that, or he didn't care; maybe to him, it was merely a natural function of the body. It was this power of concentration that made him a great star.

About six weeks into the shooting of *The Scalphunters*, we were coming up on the day when they were going to film a scene of me being shot and

Picerni and his wife Marie at the Audie Murphy Museum. In his autobiography Steps to Stardom, *he wrote that the number 11 was always important in his life, and predicted he'd die on the 11th. He died on the 12th of January...in 2011.*

killed by Burt, my last scene in the picture. After that, I was scheduled to go home. One day I said to Burt, "I've got to talk to you," and he said, "Okay, let's take a walk." As we strolled through the woods, I told him I thought it'd be much more effective if he shot and killed Dabney Coleman instead of me. I told him that, story-wise, I had a good reason for that, but actually I just wanted to get another few weeks work (the picture still had four weeks of shooting to go). I was having a lot of fun with Telly, he and Burt and I were playing golf on our days off — I didn't want to be killed off and sent home. I wanted them to kill off Dabney Coleman and send *him* home! Anyway, I told Burt my bogus "story reason" why my character should continue to live and Dabney's should die, and as we walked through the woods, Burt thought about it and thought about it. Finally said, "You know something? You might be right. Let me discuss it with Sydney." Well, he did speak to Sydney, but what I didn't know was that Dabney was Sydney's tennis teacher! To make a long story short, Burt came back to me and said, "Sorry, Paul, Sydney didn't go for it," so I ended up getting killed and going home. It was a phony "story reason" and Sydney saw right through it. But Burt didn't dismiss it, he actually thought about it. Burt was good to me.

When I got back from Mexico, Dr. Saliba took me off the Diabanese pills and put me on shots of insulin. He said it would be more effective. (He was right, and I've been on insulin ever since.) It was Telly Savalas who helped me get over my depression about my condition.

When Telly was in the Army, he spent a whole year at Walter Reed Hospital in Washington, D.C., recovering from injuries suffered during the War. I know Telly had wires in his legs, and we've all seen the shriveled-up forefinger of his right hand. Although I questioned him many times, he never told me how it happened, he would always sidestep it. I've since asked his brother Gus, and still never got the true story. Telly would always say, "Oh, I'll tell ya about it someday." He never did. That was the mystery of Telly. He never gave you it all; he kept you wanting more. That's part of what made him a great actor.

Ann Robinson
CELEBRATES
JOHNNY CARPENTER

Actress Ann Robinson astride a horse in actor-filmmaker Johnny Carpenter's made-for-television The Rimrocker. *Robinson found this long-missing (and wrinkled and emulsion-damaged) photo in her Elysian Park, California, home during the excavation that followed an October 2011 fire that badly damaged its upper floors. It took more than 70 firefighters, aided by two water-dropping helicopters, to knock down the blaze.*

Actress Ann Robinson's claim to fame is that she starred in The War of the Worlds, *one of the top-grossing films of 1953 and a Hall of Fame title in the sci-fi genre. Her career began, however, in the much more down-to-earth Western genre, as a result of a late-1940s chance encounter with John Carpenter. Then a B-Western supporting actor and bit player, Carpenter turned the pretty teenager into a cowgirl in real life and then in reel life, starting her down the trail to a Hollywood acting career. In this interview, she shares some heartwarming memories of the late Mr. Carpenter.*

ANN ROBINSON: I was 18 or 19 when I first met Johnny Carpenter. One afternoon my mother and I went to the Broadway Hollywood, a department store on Hollywood and Vine. In those days, once you pulled into the parking lot, the car was parked *for* you. I was driving, and as I got out, I saw a uniformed man coming over to park the car and I said, "My Lord, you're Johnny Carpenter!" Now [2006], all these years later, I do not recall any of the B Westerns I'd seen him in but I must have seen a *lot* of them because I recognized him *immediately*, with such *glee*. I was so happy to meet him.

Of course, he was very, very flattered. We started talking, and I guess because of my love of Westerns, he invited me to come over to a private riding stable, in the Los Feliz area of Los Angeles, where celebrities and other very wealthy people boarded their horses, and where he boarded his horse Patterfoot. Evidently he worked there, in addition to his car-parking job, because otherwise I don't know why he would have a horse there; he was not a wealthy man. He must have managed or taken care of the place.

In those days, you could ride horses through Griffith Park, where they had bridle paths everywhere. I'd grown up riding on an English saddle, and Johnny said, "I think we'd better make a cowboy out of you." He taught me how to ride Western style on Patterfoot, which was *wonderful*. I already had what they refer to as a great "seat" on a saddle, I could set a saddle, so I had no trouble at all learning to ride Western. Incidentally, Patterfoot wasn't an ordinary horse: Johnny had trained it, and so it was a very easy-to-ride, very responsive horse.

Johnny was very interested in handicapped people and blind people and, up until he passed away [in February 2003], he taught them how to be around animals and how to ride horses. Even when I first met him, he was involved with handicapped people. He had a group called the Blind Rhythm Riders, boys in their 20s or maybe even their 30s, that he was teaching to ride. They also played Western music. One day Johnny decided to gather enough money together to make a "movie" on these blind boys.

I had never done *anything* in front of a camera, but when he offered me a part, I thought it'd be a hoot. At that age, nothing scares you, so I said, "Sure, I'll do it. I'd *love* to!" It was called *The Rimrocker* and it was 35mm black-and-white. Johnny was the leading man, I was the leading lady and all our friends were in the movie. Like Andy Andrews, who had a nightclub on Manchester and Figueroa called the Red Feather that would

This page, facing page: Ann Robinson and Johnny Carpenter in Carpenter's late-1940s indie production The Rimrocker.

introduce black stars. I saw Nat "King" Cole make his Los Angeles debut singing there. Anyway, Johnny got all his friends together to be the actors in *The Rimrocker*, so *[laughs]* we all worked for nothing! Two of the bad guys were Andy and the cook at his nightclub — a wonderful cook. Boy, he had the best salad dressing!

We shot at either the Warner Brothers Ranch or Iverson's Ranch or...I don't know. *One* of the ranches out in the Valley that studios used to use to make Westerns. The plot was the typical thing, the stagecoach got robbed and Johnny and the Blind Rhythm Riders went out and caught the bad guys and brought 'em to justice and recovered the money or the gold or whatever it was they stole. And at the end they played some music.

When they were on horseback, the Blind Rhythm Riders were on horses that were tied together and Johnny led them. In one shot I had to come riding into the scene, hollering that the stagecoach was robbed. Johnny said, "When we do this shot, I want you to ride at full gallop. Then I want you to set this horse's rear end down on the ground, and I want you off and running next to the horse by the time the horse stops." Well,

of *course [laughs]!* The scene was not rehearsed because you don't know what animals are going to do — and I guess they didn't know what *I* was going to do, either! I slid that horse in, was off that horse and running, and ran into Johnny's arms screaming and crying about the stagecoach. We did it in one take. The cameraman was so shocked and surprised that I did it so perfectly.

The Rimrocker was a half-hour thing, fun to do. It was shown on television a couple of times, and it was seen by a neighbor of mine who was a grip in the studios. After he saw it, he said, "My God, this girl can not only ride, she can act!" He had a friend who was a stunt rider and a stuntman, Cliff Lyons, and he told Cliff about me. Well, Cliff got me into stunt work. The woman who was the head of Universal casting, Jonny Rennick, owed Cliff a favor, so he said, "I want an Extras Guild card for this girl, because I want to get her into the Screen Actors Guild." In those days, if you had one card, you could join another union. That's how I got started as a stunt girl and as an extra, through Johnny Carpenter and Cliff Lyons and Yakima Canutt. My absolutely first *movie* was a Roddy McDowall Western called *Black Midnight* [1949], which we shot up at Lone Pine. I was the stunt girl for the leading lady [Lyn Thomas], who couldn't ride. She would run real fast behind the barn, and then when the horse came

Ann Robinson and Johnny Carpenter in The Rimrocker.

out with somebody *on* it, it was *me [laughs]!* I was on the horse behind the barn, out of sight, waiting for her, and a few seconds after she came around the corner, away I went! The director, Budd Boetticher, bless his heart, he was my ruination in movies. He was teaching bullfighting to Roddy McDowall and I just was so fascinated, I had to know everything there was *about* it. And then what did I do, a few years later? I ran off to Mexico [in 1957] and married the famous matador Jaime Bravo, and had two sons. That was the end of my movie career!

Stunt-wise, I was also in *Frenchie* [1950] with Joel McCrea and sweet Shelley Winters. Some other stunt people and I rode in a buckboard that was going down a hill lickety-split. One of the others was driving, and I was dressed as Shelley. Then I doubled her, riding in a stagecoach that was being chased fast down a hill. They were not anticipating the stagecoach overturning, but it missed a turn and *did*. I had the best time meeting Joel McCrea and Shelley, it was a lovely experience. A year ago, August the 18th [2005], my son Estefan and my husband Val and I were invited to her Beverly Hills home for her 85th birthday party. She was precious, it was a wonderful party and it was fun to be able to remind her that I was her stunt girl on *Frenchie*. She said to Estefan, "Boy, your mother made me

To publicize her most famous movie, 1953's The War of the Worlds, *Robinson submitted to becoming a "Lady from Mars." Wally Westmore applies green-gold paint.*

look good in that movie," and then she held up the *Frenchie* poster we'd brought to the party for her to autograph, and she said, "Wasn't I a *dish?*"

None of this would have happened without *The Rimrocker* and without Johnny Carpenter. He was such a sincere human being and just a loving, loving man. And he was from "the old school." He lived in an apartment house on Vermont Avenue and in the early days, if I were with him when

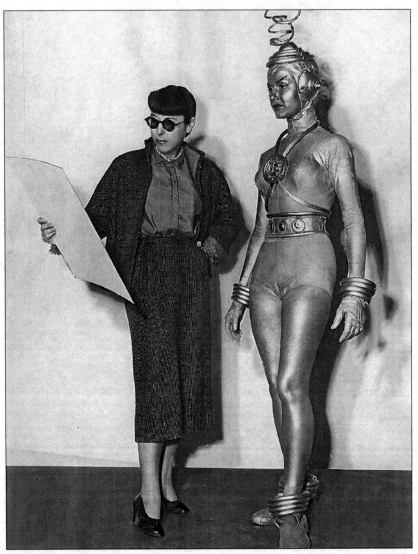

Costume designer Edith Head (who dreamed up this stunt) joins Ann as a "Lady from Mars" to promote The War of the Worlds *(1953).*

he had to go to the apartment, he made me stay in the car because, he said, "it would not look right" if I, a young single woman, came up to his apartment. And his hands were strong — massive, massive palms. I'm sure if he gripped you, he could break a bone. His hands were almost like cowhide, they were so rough and so strong. He wasn't a very tall man — I'm 5'6" and he was a little bit taller than I, maybe 5'8". But he just had a wonderful, kind face and attitude.

The beauteous and bodacious Ann Robinson today.

I used to regularly be at his stables, where he had Patterfoot and then a new horse named Sugarfoot. When he got a third horse and he asked, "What shall we name it?," I said, "How 'bout *Pussy*foot?" He thought that was a little vulgar, and at the time I didn't understand *why* it was vulgar *[laughs]!* But he sorta frowned on that suggestion, and we ended up calling the third horse Fleetfoot. We were also in a lot of little local parades and things like that, on horseback. The Blind Rhythm Riders and the other friends of ours who were in *The Rimrocker* all rode in parades together. These "parades" were all of, like, two or three blocks, like a big Christmas parade in your neighborhood, but we had fun. But what was *really* funny was the fact that we had no transportation for the horses, so we had to ride them from the Los Feliz stables *to* the parade, and back when it was over. *That* distance was a lot longer than the parade itself. We were in our *own* parade going down Los Feliz Boulevard!

Once I started working a lot, started doing things at Paramount, I saw less of Johnny, but we did keep in touch. Eventually he had his own ranch [John Carpenter's Heaven on Earth Ranch for Handicapped Children]. It was at different locations over the years, for financial reasons, or because leases ran out, or whatever. Back in the late '80s, when his ranch was at Hansen Dam in the Valley, I visited and he showed me around. It was adorable, it looked just like an old town that you would see in a Western movie. Everything was sorta dusty and dirty and looked so authentic!

There was a wild west show and stagecoaches and campfires and cookouts, and all the underprivileged and handicapped children loved to pretend that they were *in* Westerns and doing cowboy things. Doing that for these kids was all he was interested in.

When I read about Johnny's [February 2003] passing in *The Los Angeles Times*, I was so pleased that there was a wonderful picture of him and a quite-long, lovely obituary. What went through my mind when I found out that he had died was the fact that he was totally responsible for everything that's happened to me. Definitely, he was responsible for my career. Absolutely. If it had not been for him, I don't know *how* I would have gotten into movies. Couldn't sing, couldn't dance, couldn't do anything! With all the Western film festivals that they have today, I wish somebody would recognize him and honor him, because I *do* believe he deserves it. I think he was as important as Bob Steele and people like that. Gee, I wish Johnny were still around. What a wonderful, caring, giving man he was.

Jo Ann Sayers
SEES *THE LIGHT OF WESTERN STARS*

Jo Ann Sayers, Victor Jory and Noah Beery, Jr., in The Light of Western Stars *(1940).*

The leading lady in Paramount's The Light of Western Stars, *Jo Ann Sayers (birth name: Miriam Lucille Lilygren) was born in Seattle, Washington. Named after the Biblical Moses' dancer-sister Miriam, she danced as a child, took violin and piano lessons and acted in school plays. She attended the University of Washington with hopes of becoming a lawyer, but was drawn to the drama department instead. An agent "spotted" her and offered her a chance to make a screen test, which in turn led to Sayers' brief but busy run in MGM Hollywood features and shorts (and, later, the Broadway stage; she played the title role in the hit* My Sister Eileen). *Now widowed and residing in New Jersey, Sayers here recalls her one and only Western.*

JO ANN SAYERS: When I was offered the part in *The Light of Western Stars* [1940], I took it because I liked the part — I guess that was one reason — but also, it was a *job*. In *all* of my acting career, all I was really ever interested in was just working, and I *liked* to work. The thing about the movie I remember best was Lone Pine, where it was filmed, and seeing those great big, "famous" rocks that you see in so many Western movies. They'd told me, "It's going to be chilly at night," so I took my pink satin comforter with me *[laughs]*. My mother was with me, too, and we had a very good time, enjoyed it. Mother hadn't been on the set a lot with me at MGM, but she did go on location with me on *Western Stars*, and that was really fun. We stayed at some little hotel there. It might have been on that movie that Mother got

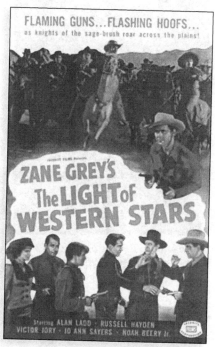

Sayers co-starred as a Boston socialite in The Light of Western Stars, *fourth screen version of a Zane Grey novel. "[The story] is decidedly dated, straining with age in its dramatics," a* Variety *critic carped.*

nicknamed Sonya because she was beautiful — very dark hair, big blue eyes and so forth. They thought she looked like a Sonya so they called her Sonya Sayers *[laughs]*, which was sort of fun. I have a handkerchief of hers that I just came across again the other day, with red embroidery on it, SONYA SAYERS. When they named her that, she loved it and had some handkerchiefs made with that name on it!

Harry "Pop" Sherman, the producer, wasn't around; I think I met him at some point but I don't now remember where. He had a nice reputation, unlike *some* other types around Hollywood. Like at MGM maybe. Mr.

Jo Ann Sayers, from her MGM movie days (above) and from Broadway's long-running My Sister Eileen *(facing page).*

You-Know-Who [studio boss Louis B. Mayer]. I did quite a few things at Metro, but when my contract was to be renewed, he called me into his office and started chasing me around the desk! He didn't catch me *[laughs]*, so my contract was terminated!

The director on *Western Stars*, Lesley Selander, was a really nice guy. And Ellen Corby, who was our script girl, went on to do *so* much as an actress herself, *The Waltons*, etc. I liked her very much and I've never forgotten her. She just was a very real person, a very nice person. Years after *Western Stars*, when I first started seeing her in movies, I said *[gasps]*, "There's Ellen Corby...!" She was very nice; as a matter of fact, *every*body was, the whole cast and the whole crew. So it was fun.

As for the riding, I loved that. When I was very young, I spent many summers in Wyoming, the whole family used to go there in the summer, because some very close friends of ours had a gold mine in a tiny, tiny little area called Atlantic City. We visited our friends there, they had a daughter about my age and we did a lot of riding and had a great time. I was a young teenager, only worried about whether my nails were painted and my hair was in place, even though the population of the town was *nine [laughs]*. We'd ride out and explore, reach down and pick up an

arrowhead or something like that, visit other people's homes. It was very easy fun riding, my two sisters and I and our friend. So I had no problem riding a horse in *Western Stars*. Of course I had doubles who did all the fast riding.

Noah Beery was a darling guy. We called him Pidge, that was his nickname. He was very sweet. He kinda got stuck with that type of role

Sayers in yet another MGM publicity pose.

[the sidekick-best friend-nice guy] for some reason or other, but he was very good at it, I thought. In *Western Stars* he *was* a Mexican nice guy and gave up his life at the end.

Victor Jory kept pretty much to himself. I really only knew him through working in scenes together. Which was fine. Years ago, when we had a little family reunion — my mother came from Kentucky — we all met in Louisville, where a cousin of my mother's lived. And living across the street from [the cousin] was John Jory, the son of Victor; John ran the famous Actors Theatre of Louisville. We went over and visited John, and he gave me a couple of posters from *Light of Western Stars*, which was very nice of him. Victor had died several years before.

Q: I thought Jory did a good job in the saloon fight scene in Western Stars.

I watched part of that being shot. I wasn't around for *all* the scenes, of course, but I remember watching part of *that* scene. If you'll notice, in some of the scenes, his back is to the camera, so I think there was somebody filling in for him. I remember, too, that he had the most gorgeous horse [a palomino] in the movie, absolutely beautiful. Oh, and the ring that he puts on my finger in the movie? My daughter Eileen has it now,

Two late-in-life shots of the still-beautiful Jo Ann Sayers. The one on the right was taken on her 93rd birthday (October 22, 2011), less than a month before she passed away.

but for years and years it sat around here, and I wore it a little bit for a while. It was a nice ring, a silver horseshoe with a spider vein turquoise in the center.

The town where some of the scenes take place — that, of course, was not Lone Pine, that was just a street set someplace, a set that was used a lot in the Westerns. One time while we were waiting for cameras to be set up and so forth, I walked into one of the little buildings. Some were real buildings and some were fake, and I walked into one of the real ones and there was nothing there but an old Victrola. I thought, "That's interesting," so I lifted the lid, and I disturbed a whole family of mice *[laughs]* — the tiniest, most adorable baby mice. I felt *so mean* — the larger mice ran, and the mother ran, and the babies were just "lost," bumping around. So

I closed it up again. Whether she ever got back in there, I don't know. Almost 60 years later, I still feel bad about that! Oh, and I remember my last costume, the last dress that I wore in the movie. I just hated that dress! It was Hollywood's idea of what breasts should look like, and they were pointed — the dress was *built* to point *[laughs]*. I was embarrassed wearing it, I didn't feel comfortable in it. However, I thought the other dresses were sort of fun.

Did you know that they changed the title of that movie for television? They called it *Border Renegade*. One day I was told that *Border Renegade* was going to be shown on television. Well, I couldn't be home for it, but I told my kids [her daughter Eileen and son Tony] and the person who was taking care of them. They watched it, and according to the report I got later, my son, who was five or six, looked at it with "a face of doubt" *all* the way through. They told him, "That's Mommy!," and he just watched and watched, but he didn't believe it. Then at the very end of the movie, there was this big kiss, this big clinch, and that cinched it for him, he declared *[Sayers speaks in a loud, indignant voice]*, "*That's* not Mommy. She wouldn't *do* a thing like that!" I just thought that was wonderful!

I had the hardest time getting my own copy of *Light of Western Stars*. You've heard of Publishers Clearing House? They kept sending me their catalogues, and a couple of years ago I opened one and was zooming through all the odds and ends, and I saw a video advertised called *Light of Western Stars* for sale, and it had my picture with Victor Jory, embracing — they'd taken our picture together right off one of the posters. But when I read the little blurb that appeared alongside it, it mentioned a lot of people in the cast that I'd never heard of! So I sent for it, and it was totally different. It was a version of *Light of Western Stars* that must have been made in the '20s sometime, with a totally different cast — and so dark that you could hardly see it! So I called my lawyer, and the Publishers Clearing House was contacted. They eventually claimed they'd destroyed all of them, or something like that, and I left it at that! But eventually I did get a copy of "my" movie, and watched it again, and I thought it was pretty good. It was interesting, it was fun to relive it — and I didn't think I was as bad as I *thought* I was going to be *[laughs]*.

I have a very busy, happy life today. I ballroom dance, which I love; I've competed a couple of times and I showcase twice a year. And I still get fan letters, and I can't believe it. So many of these people say what big fans of the old movies they are. Which I can understand. When *I* look at old movies on television, I *must* say, the dialogue is so much better, and there's no hi-tech action junk that is just distracting.

Paul Wurtzel
ON BEL-AIR WESTERNS

Having a Hollywood movie producer for a dad does have its little perks!
A chip off 20th Century-Fox producer Sol M. Wurtzel's old block, young
Paul Wurtzel lounges poolside with (clockwise from lower left) Mary Healy,
Lynn Bari, Elyse Knox and Marjorie Weaver.

One of the best things about the 1950s Westerns made by Howard W. Koch-Aubrey Schenck's Bel-Air Productions was their use of great locations in Kanab, Utah. Paul Wurtzel, assistant director on several of these outdoor shows, here recalls the fun and the challenges of the days of fast-and-furious shooting in "Utah's Little Hollywood."

PAUL WURTZEL: Back in the days when Howard Koch was an assistant director, he worked in Kanab on some big Western feature, and he loved it because the studio built these wonderful sets: a fort that they spent a fortune on, and a small Western town. They were well-built and they looked *real* and, after shooting the picture, the studio left 'em there. Howard, when *he* became a producer and started making Westerns, figured it'd be great to use those sets and so they started writing some of their Westerns *for* those sets.

The way I got to work with Howard on his shows was, I was in a serious automobile accident and was really busted up. Finally I got well enough to go back to work, but I couldn't really walk well, I had to use crutches. That's when Howard brought me into Bel-Air Productions by giving me a job as a location manager so that I didn't have to do the amount of walking an assistant does. The first job I had with him, they were up at Kanab doing a Western and I was going to be the location manager. Actually, Howard didn't need a location manager in Kanab, *he* knew where everything was up there and he'd pick all the locations and that was *it*, but he did it just to give me a job. They were already in Kanab and I was about to come up from Los Angeles, and he called me and he said, "There's no Chinese restaurant up here and everybody wants Chinese food!" He told me to get the food at Ah Fong, a Chinese restaurant in Beverly Hills run by an actor who was in the Charlie Chan movies, Benson Fong; Benson knew Howard very well. I told Benson that Howard wanted all this Chinese food, the spare ribs and the shrimp and everything, and that I'd be driving it up to Utah. He made a ton of stuff and we put it in my trunk with a lot of dry ice, and I had to drive up — and it was about six or eight hours, a *long* drive. I got in my car in Beverly Hills with this Chinese food and dry ice, and when I got to Vegas I found a place that sold dry ice ('cause most of it had melted by then) and loaded the trunk with *more* dry ice and took off again, and I got up to Kanab at just about dinnertime. It wasn't terrific food after all that *[laughs]* but they heated it up and ate it, and Howard was so happy to get it.

That was my first Bel-Air picture, and then when I got well enough, he switched me over to assistant director and I stayed on and did a lot of the rest of 'em. It was tough to get up there in those days because Kanab only had a little dirt runway for an airstrip. You'd have to fly into Cedar City, which is way downstate, and then bus everybody up. Finally Kanab made the runway longer so you could land a DC3 on it, but there were no lights on the strip. So you had to come in in the morning and leave before it got dark.

We'd stay at Parry Lodge, a huge, wonderful motel-like place with terrific food. It was mostly Mormons up there. There was some agriculture...

Cast and crew of Tomahawk Trail *converge for a giant group shot.*

not much. Mostly it was cattle people and horses and things. And the people were "starving"! Therefore, when the movie companies came in and spent a fortune, the Kanab people loved them. When Howard went there to do pictures on the cheap, he got a lot of help from the locals, who remembered him from the earlier picture [which he assistant-directed]. He was good to the people, he was very generous, hiring them all to work as extras and all kinds of jobs like that. Howard was very likable and he always tried to help the little guy, and *they* bent over backwards to give him anything he wanted, in order to keep getting us up there. So we made a lot of those six- and seven-day Western features there, and we used a lot of livestock, and we even brought Indians in from Tuba City, which is down some place in Arizona. So those were the reasons that they went up there, for the fort and Western town, and the people were terrific, and the beautiful scenery — they had the red Utah dirt, like Bryce Canyon. And the Indians were the real thing! Within driving distance from our "headquarters" [Parry Lodge], there was everything we wanted, and everything was half-price [compared to Hollywood], or *less* than half.

Q: There was everything everybody wanted — except a drink!

Yeah, because it was Mormon. Well, we'd go over the border, which was about four miles from Kanab, across into Arizona. Right on the border there was a big bar-restaurant called the Buckskin Café where you could get all the booze you wanted, and some of the guys would bring booze back. So that was good! Also, a little bit outside of town there was a place that was like a nightclub that they built inside this cave, and they'd have dances. I'm sure *they* served booze. Howard had a thing about ice cream — ice cream and Chinese food were what he lived on. So a few of us — like, the cameraman, the director and a couple of other guys — Howard would always make us walk down the street with him, two or three blocks, to the Frosty Freeze and he'd buy us all ice cream. *That* was "the big thrill" *[laughs]!*

We'd shoot every day and, in the beginning, the film would be flown back down to Hollywood where it was processed, and then they sent it back up to Kanab where we'd run it. I think we looked at the dailies in a movie

On top of working on movies, Wurtzel also assisted-directed television episodes. He's pictured here on the set of MGM's 1950s mystery series The Thin Man.

theater there. But we didn't do that too long because directors like Reggie LeBorg [*War Drums* and *The Dalton Girls*, both 1957] would see the dailies and want to redo something and Howard would say, "Forget it!" So they quit running the dailies *[laughs]!* LeBorg was okay, but kind of a dreamer, always trying to do something different. There's nothing wrong with that, and he had good taste, better than *most* of 'em. But he was always trying to make a better thing out of each picture and I'd have to keep reminding him [about the need to stay on schedule]. In *The Dalton Girls* there was one scene where he was trying to pose the girls so their bosoms were sticking out into the lens; he was fiddling around and wasting a lot of time trying to get some

sex into it. But he would get the pictures done. Lesley Selander [director of *Revolt at Fort Laramie* and *Tomahawk Trail*, 1957] was terrific. He was a big, tall guy, rugged, and he knew what he was doing. He would hike all over the landscape looking for just the right spot to shoot and you'd have to follow him with all the equipment. Whenever [the crew] would hear that Les was going to direct a picture, the reaction would be, "Oh, Christ, *Les*? Now we're gonna be running all over the place!" *[laughs]* He was a good guy.

In *Tomahawk Trail*, we had the baseball player from the Dodgers, Chuck Connors. He was crazy — literally. I don't know what was wrong with him. He was a nice enough guy to work with, but get a few drinks in him and he'd want to pick fights with everybody and

Wurtzel remembers Tomahawk Trail *star Chuck Connors as being "crazy — literally."*

stuff like that. He'd get wild-eyed — it was really strange! He got in a big scrape in the dining room one night, at dinner. There were other people eating there, tourists and stuff, so one great big Teamster driver grabbed Connors and kinda shuffled him out of the room before he could start breaking up the furniture *[laughs]*. Lex Barker [*War Drums*] was fine, he got his work done. At the time, he was married to Lana Turner, and *she* came up and just sat around up there. Lana Turner was lovely, I loved her, she was terrific. I never worked with her on anything but I know she came up the hard way and that she wouldn't take any crap from anybody, but she was real sweet. She was pregnant at that time but then she lost the baby.

There was an Indian that Howard hired to do a part in one of the pictures, I can't remember which one, but he'd always get drunk and disappear. And it was one of the more prominent parts in the picture! So Howard got the sheriff, who was a tough little son of a bitch, to lock this Indian up at night in jail so he couldn't take off and get drunk, and so we'd have him the next morning *[laughs]!* The sheriff was named Lynnard Johnson, he was about 5'7" and just a tough guy. He'd been a hero in World War II and then came back and was the sheriff there. His size didn't make much difference, everybody really listened to him when he said something!

Fort Bowie [1958] I don't remember at all except that in it we had Ben Johnson, a terrific guy and a great cowboy — one of the *real* cowboys. He was a cowboy in Oklahoma and a terrific roper and a rodeo guy, and then he became a pretty big star. He won an Oscar, even! And he was a very *sexy* guy, women fell all over him. We had to shoot and finish *Fort Bowie* so they could get on the DC3 and take off before the sun set, because there were no runway lights. Howard was directing, and we finished at 2:30 or 3:00 and rushed back to Parry Lodge and everybody got packed, and we had a bus out in front of the main lodge building. At that point, my job was to make sure that everybody got on the bus and got out to the airport. Well, I got our people on the bus, probably 18 of 'em, and Ben Johnson was the only guy missing. So I ran to his little bungalow room, and he was in *bed*. I said, "Jesus, Ben, get up! We gotta go!" He said, "No, I think I'm gonna stay here. I got this waitress that's gonna come over tonight..." *[laughs]* Really! He said, "Don't worry, I'll get home, that's *my* problem. You guys go, and I'm staying here." I argued with him for another few moments, and then I ran back out — and the bus was *gone*! Oh, shit. One of the guys who supplied us with all the wagons and horses was Fay Hamblin, who was famous up in Kanab, he was the go-to guy if you needed anything. He was a real cowboy, a guy about 60 I guess. He saw me and he kinda smiled and he said, "Howard came out to the bus and looked and he started screaming, 'Where the hell is Wurtzel?! If we wait, we're not gonna be able to take the plane up, we'll have to keep everybody over another day and pay 'em!" So Howard jumped in the bus and they all took off for the airfield! Fay said, "You come on, I'll drive you out there." So we went flying down the road and we got there, and the bus was empty and the plane was on the field and everybody was on it. I jumped out and ran up to the plane as they were just closing the door on this old DC3. Aubrey Schenck was sitting in there, looking out one of the windows, and he saw me and he started...you know how you say "Shame on you!" with your finger *[laughs]*? He did that, but he was grinning. Howard came flying out, and he chewed me out like I'd never been chewed out before! Oh, *God*, he gave it to me! It turned out that somebody had told Howard that I had gone back into the lodge to take a *shower [laughs]* — some guy really shafted me! I said, "For Christ's sake, I was trying to get Ben Johnson and he wouldn't go!" Howard was *so* mad, I'd never seen him like that! He really chewed my ass out, while Aubrey was sitting there making the "Shame on you!" gesture and grinning. He thought it was so funny! Well, they finally got the goddamn plane off just as the sun was setting. Holy Christ!

Making those Bel-Air pictures was a great experience. I'll tell you one last, quick story. Aubrey Schenck died first [in 1999] and was cremated, and then when Howard passed away two years later, *he* was cremated. And Howard's wish was to have his ashes scattered over Kanab, Utah. He loved Kanab and they loved him: By making these cheap pictures there at a time when Kanab was not doing too well financially, Howard gave a lot of employment to the local people. So they thought Howard was a great guy — which he *was*. Anyway, nobody could believe that Howard wanted to have his

Wurtzel's main memory of making Fort Bowie *in Kanab is of almost being* left behind *in Kanab!*

ashes scattered over Kanab, they thought he'd want to be buried out here, but no, he wanted his ashes scattered over the fort set. When Aubrey's widow Florie heard about this, she said, "I've got Aubrey's ashes. Why don't we send him up and scatter *both* of their ashes out at the same time over Kanab?" So their two sons went there, Howard's son Hawk and Aubrey's son, writer-producer George Schenck, and they approached Mickey Whiting, a fellow we used to work with when we were on location there. Mickey, who owned a lumber company and also had his own plane, said, "Oh, sure, I'll fly you up and we'll go over the fort and you can scatter the ashes" — and that's what they did.

Well, after the plane landed, along came a flock of geese from Canada, flying south for the winter. This huge flock came over and they circled the fort where the ashes had just been scattered, and then they continued on their way. The natives up there said, "We've never seen anything like that. We see the geese all the time at this time of year, flying south — but never before have they ever stopped to circle the fort." I know the story because I talk to both of the women [Mrs. Koch and Mrs. Schenck] and the sons, and they told me about it. It's kind of an interesting story. It's almost like one of those miraculous things.

INDEX

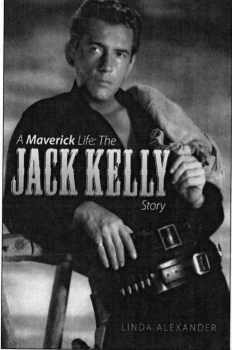

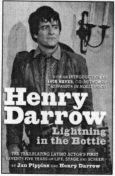